MORE CHICKEN BREASTS

91 new and classic recipes for the fairest part of the fowl

BY DIANE ROZAS

A Particular Palate Cookbook™
Crown Trade Paperbacks
New York

This book is for Anita and Richard Gottehrer.

A Particular Palate Cookbook

Copyright © 1991, 1996 by Diane Rozas

Published by Crown Trade Paperbacks, 201 East 50th Street, New York, New York 10022. Member of the Crown Publishing Group.

Originally published by Harmony Books, a division of Crown Publishers, Inc. in 1991.

Random House, Inc. New York, Toronto, London, Sydney, Auckland

CROWN TRADE PAPERBACKS, PARTICULAR PALATE, and colophons are trademarks of Crown Publishers, Inc.

Printed in The United States of America

Library of Congress Cataloging-in-Publication Data

Rozas, Diane.

More Chicken Breasts / by Diane Rozas.—1st ed.
   "A Particular palate cookbook series"— Includes index.
   1. Cookery (Chicken)   I. Title.
   TX750.5.C45R69   1990
   641.6'65–dc20   90-36191
                   CIP
ISBN 0-517-88706-1

10 9 8 7 6 5 4 3 2 1

Second Edition

Contents

Introduction

Recently, in the mail, I received a letter from a friend requesting a new copy of *Chicken Breasts: 116 new and classic recipes for the fairest part of the fowl* (my first book on the ever-popular topic, published in 1985). Accompanying the letter was a well-used copy of the book. It was in unspeakable condition: the paper and plastic on the front cover had separated, and the plastic was peeling off. My heart sank as I stared at this abused little book. Large dried-on stains of what appeared to be barbecue sauce made it look as though Count Dracula had taken it along on one of his midnight escapades. Grease splatters and general kitchen stains also appeared like battle scars . . . everywhere. What had this book gone through in its short, two-and-a-half-year life in the kitchen of my friend, Deanna Lund? The back cover was yet another story. The book had been left on the stove, by a burner flame, which "blackened" it like a piece of Paul Prudhomme fish. At least it was keeping up with the latest food trends. The inside pages were in the same incredible condition. Though dirty and stained, suddenly I realized that every minute I had put into the creation of this book had been worth it because I could easily

tell which recipes were a hit. Herb and French Mustard–Basted Chicken Breasts had become a standard, by the looks of the well-worn pages. Another obvious favorite, Kung Pao Chicken, was totally stained with droplets of soy sauce. And the Creole Curry Chicken Breasts recipe also showed signs of frequent use. Yes, I replaced this tattered and stained book with a brand new one.

As I thumbed through those well-worn pages, I began to consider how times had changed in the food world, how different the recipes I prefer to make today are from those of just five years ago, when the first book was published.

My taste for hot and spicier foods has been pulled right along with the southwestern and Thai food crazes that have heated up over the past few years. And diet food, in my book (figuratively speaking), no longer consists of lettuce leaves and a plain poached chicken breast. Now the wonders of Spa Cuisine are showing up in my kitchen with great frequency. Grilling has become a primary style of cooking, bringing with it new and more interesting marinades and basting sauces. And who hasn't tried "grazing" through a buffet, taking bits of this and that, passing up a whole meal in favor of a variety of incredibly unusual nibbles? Salads seem to have escaped the ubiquitous "summer season" role, becoming a year-round favorite with the business crowd at "power lunches" from Washington, D.C., to Manhattan to the hills of Hollywood. And speaking of power, let us not ignore the importance of microwave cooking these days, or the fact that chicken breasts are most compatible with this method of cooking.

Though these new attitudes toward food prevail throughout my own recipe files, the primary reasons for serving chicken breasts, whether it be in my kitchen, in your home, or at a restaurant, will never change: they are healthy—low in calories and cholesterol, inexpensive, and quick-cooking—an important consideration in today's busier-than-ever world.

Here are eighty new and tantalizing chicken breast recipes, from starters to entrées, that reflect the taste and lifestyle of the 1990s.

Preparing Chicken Breasts

A few simple suggestions will put some extra money in your pocket as well as allow you to enjoy the most tender, tastiest chicken breast dishes you can cook.

BUYING CHICKEN BREASTS Look for large, plump breasts, free of bruises. Pick only those with a well-rounded breast and a flexible backbone. Use your nose to determine absolute freshness—the breast should have no odor whatsoever. Color is not a factor in flavor, just a reflection of the different chicken feeds used throughout the country.

BONING AND SKINNING A WHOLE CHICKEN BREAST Though skinned and boned chicken breasts are readily available in packages of two or three, skinning and boning the breasts at home can save as much as several dollars per pound. Butcher-boned and -skinned breasts sometimes top five dollars per pound. Also, the chicken breasts will remain more moist, fresh, and succulent when prepared just prior to cooking, because the bone and skin act as a natural encasement, preventing the delicate meat from drying out—the greatest detriment to its final flavor and texture.

Once you've had a little practice, boning and skinning is a simple process, taking only a few minutes. Freezing the chicken breasts for half an hour before beginning will make this task even easier.

1. Place the whole breast on a work surface, skin side up. Peel the skin back and off. Trim away any remaining bits of skin and fat.

2. Using a very sharp boning knife with a flexible blade (see page 11), insert the tip at one end of the breastbone, between the rib cage and the meat. Keeping the knife as close as possible to the rib cage, work it along the edge of the breast from one end to the other. Separate the meat from the bone to the depth of 2 inches. (At this point the breast meat will still be attached in the center to the breastbone, on both sides.)

3. With the knife and your fingers, scrape or push the meat toward the breastbone until it is *completely* loosened from the rib cage but still attached to the breastbone.

4. Scrape and push the meat away from the breastbone, being careful not to tear the meat. Remove the breast meat.

SPLITTING A CHICKEN BREAST AND REMOVING THE TENDON

1. Using your sharp boning knife, slice the breast in half following the center indentation, where it was attached to the bone.

2. Slip the point of the boning knife under one end of the white tendon running along the underside of the breast and lift the tendon away from the meat, holding an end of the tendon with one hand while lifting and scraping the meat away carefully.

FLATTENING CHICKEN BREASTS Flatten chicken breasts to a uniform thickness with a flat-headed metal pounder or wooden mallet. Put the breasts, skin side up, between two sheets of waxed paper or plastic wrap and carefully pound to the required thickness with light, even strokes.

STORING CHICKEN BREASTS At this point, if you are not cooking the prepared breasts immediately, wrap them tightly in individual plastic sandwich bags or several layers of plastic wrap, to keep them from drying out, and refrigerate or freeze until needed.

Q: How much does a chicken breast weigh?

A: The chicken breasts called for in these recipes are of average size, weighing 12 to 14 ounces (the whole breast) after skinning and boning, or about a pound each with the bone and skin on). However, depending on the size of the breasts and the appetites of those eating, one serving can be either a half or a whole breast. Recipe servings should be adjusted accordingly.

TERMS AND TECHNIQUES

Chiffonade: A technique for cutting leafy vegetables and herbs into ribbon-like strands. Roll the lettuce, spinach, collard greens, herbs, arugula, baby chicory, cabbage, and so on in a tight bundle, leaf around leaf around leaf. Holding the leaves together tightly, slice to the required thickness, usually ¼ to ½ inch. The result is a pile of curled strips. Vegetables can then be sautéed (as with spinach or collard greens) or used raw as a bed for many different types of salads.

Deglaze: A means of using the fat and pan juices to make a sauce. First pour off any excess fat. With the pan over medium-high heat add 1 cup of dry white or red table wine, cream, or stock to the bubbling juice. Cook over medium heat, stirring constantly and scraping up any browned bits left on the bottom or sides of the pan. Then add enough liquid (either wine, cream, or stock) to make the amount of sauce required. To thicken the sauce, add a beaten egg yolk mixed with a little heavy cream, making sure the heat is turned to very low. (Do not boil once the egg yolk has been added.) Strain before serving.

Julienne: A technique for making very thin strips of food—vegetables, chicken breast, citrus rind, and so forth—for either fast-cooking methods or garnishes. First cut the food into 1½-inch lengths. Pile them together and cut into very thin strips.

Reduce: A means of thickening a sauce. Cook the ingredients for a short time over high heat to decrease the amount of liquid (stock, water, wine, or cream), and strengthen the flavors.

INGREDIENTS

Bread Crumbs: Bread crumbs are either fresh or dry. For fresh bread crumbs, put 2 to 3 slices of bread in a blender or food processor, one at a time, and process until fine. For dry, leave the bread out to dry before crumbing it. Store dried bread crumbs in an airtight container.

Butter, Oil: When butter is called for, use unsalted (sweet) butter; you can always add salt to the recipe. Oils can be either virgin olive oil or vegetable oils such as safflower, corn, peanut, and clear sesame oil (not to be confused with the dark, Oriental-style oil that is called for in several of the stir-fry recipes). Oils should always be fresh, never previously used for frying.

Chicken Stock: To prepare stock, put 1 pound chicken parts—including back, neck, wings, and bones—in a heavy saucepan, along with 1 chopped carrot, 1 sliced onion, 1 celery stalk, 1 poaching bouquet (see below), 10 black peppercorns, 5 whole cloves, 5 parsley sprigs, and a large bay leaf. Cover the ingredients with 3 to 4 cups water and bring to a rapid boil. With a spoon, remove any foamy scum that collects on top of the water; reduce the heat and simmer, uncovered, for 1 hour. Strain and store in a glass jar in the refrigerator, or freeze in a plastic container. For small amounts, freeze stock in ice cube trays and then put the stock cubes in plastic freezer bags. Frozen, stock will last for up to 3 months; refrigerated, for 3 days.

Cream, Sour Cream, Crème Fraîche: When cream is called for use heavy, or whipping, cream unless otherwise specified. Sour cream should be the dairy variety; imitation does not have the delicate richness of the real thing, and it separates when heated. Crème fraîche, or French cultured cream, can be easily made with 2½ cups heavy cream and 2 tablespoons buttermilk. Mix them together and let stand for 3 to 4 hours in a warm (75° to 80° F.) area near or on the stove.

Herbs, Spices, Flavorings: Use fresh herbs whenever they are available. If they are not, make sure the dried herbs you have are aromatic and have been stored in airtight containers, away from heat and light. Black pepper should always be ground at the moment of use; its flavor dissipates quickly. Many of the following recipes require combinations of herbs and spices in partnership with butter, wine, cream, and other ingredients to enhance the flavors of the meat. Herbs and spices are also used in marinades to infuse the delicate white meat with delicious flavor before cooking. Herbs and spices should always be top quality and as fresh as possible.

Marinades: There are two types of marinades, wet and dry. Wet marinades include enough liquid to partially immerse chicken breasts before cooking and later are also used as a basting sauce. Marinades usually include a combination of herbs and spices and perhaps a small amount of oil, which is rubbed into the chicken. After combining the marinade ingredients with the chicken breast, allow enough time for the flavors to penetrate. Luckily, chicken breasts absorb flavors quickly: 1 to 4 hours. Some wet marinades, such as those with lemon juice or wine, also act as tenderizers. Liqueurs impart strong flavors, so use them sparingly.

Poaching Bouquets: Perhaps the most popular and best-known is the classic French bouquet garni, which always includes a bay leaf, fresh parsley, and thyme. Other ingredients can be added, such as a celery stalk or tops, leek greens, a fennel bulb, and garlic. Poaching bouquets can be either tied in a bundle with kitchen string or tied in a cheesecloth bag, which is a good idea for ingredients such as garlic, cloves, peppercorns, and lemon zest.

Wines and Liqueurs: Wine imparts a wonderful nutty flavor as the alcohol evaporates during the cooking process. Almost any wine or liqueur can be used in cooking chicken breasts—vermouth, red or white table wines, Madeira, Marsala, brandy, Cognac, etc.; experimentation is highly recommended. When wine or liquor is used, the alcohol should be burned off, either by flaming or rapid cooking.

EQUIPMENT

Basting Brush: For grilling or basting, a long-handled brush will help distribute a sauce or marinade over the meat's surface.

Boning Knife: A stainless-steel-coated blade made of high-carbon steel is best. The blade, 5 to 5½ inches (with a total length of about 11 inches, including the handle), should be flexible.

Mallet: A flat-edged mallet, a pounding bat, or a rolling pin is recommended for flattening chicken breasts.

Pepper Mill: Pepper is one of the essentials for properly seasoned chicken breasts. The flavor of pepper subsides almost immediately after it is ground, so commercially prepared ground pepper doesn't do much in terms of flavoring food. All pepper mills work on the same principle, so it is not necessary to invest a fortune in an imported precision-made model.

Sauté Pan, Saucepan, Baking Pan: Many of the quick and easy recipes for chicken breasts start with a simple sauté. The proper pan has a flat bottom and sides that go straight up (unlike frying pans, which have slanted or slightly rounded sides), and should be made of heavy-gauge and highly conductive metal that transmits heat evenly and steadily, without "hot spots." The best sauté pans are copper lined with tin or heavy-gauge aluminum lined with stainless steel. A good, strong handle, one that is made separately from the pan, then bolted on, is recommended. The pan should have a tight-fitting lid. Almost any saucepan can be used when one is called for, and baking dishes can be made of any ovenproof material.

Wok: A bowl-shaped low-carbon-steel Chinese pan used for the stir-fry method of cooking (see page 81 for details).

Q: How much do chicken breasts cost today?

A: According to Frank, head of the meat department at Mrs. Gooches' Natural Foods Ranch Market in Beverly Hills, California, their best breasts as of January 1991 were $3.29 per pound, bone in; $5.98 per pound for skinless and boneless breasts.

Starters

Eating in the '80s has become nibbling in the '90s.

Call them alfresco finger food, grazing fare, first courses, cocktail accompaniments, or hors d'oeuvres. Starters are plan-ahead, prepare-ahead tidbits that are appropriate passed on silver platters at wedding parties or taken in a basket to the seaside. We invented this concept (yes, you out there) when we stopped eating to live and made food fit into our lives.

Whatever these small munchies are called, they are lovely bits of flavorful and sometimes fanciful foods with chicken breasts as their main ingredient. Chicken and Cheese Quesadillas with a lively Tomato Corn Salsa on the side and Herb Rolled Chicken Breast Slices are among the delectable recipes you'll encounter in this section.

CHICKEN AND CHEESE QUESADILLAS

Long a favorite in border towns like San Diego, this quick-to-fix starter has Mexican influences. These are best served sizzling hot. Sangria or margaritas are my libation of choice.

8 servings

Salsa
½ small sweet red pepper, finely diced
½ small green pepper, finely diced
¾ cup frozen corn kernels, thawed under warm running water
2 medium plum tomatoes, peeled, seeded, and cubed
2 tablespoons minced fresh cilantro
4 medium scallions, coarsely chopped
1 tablespoon red wine vinegar
½ teaspoon ground cumin
2 tablespoons vegetable oil
Salt and freshly ground black pepper to taste

1 cup bite-size pieces of cooked chicken breast
½ cup coarsely chopped canned mild green chiles
2 cups grated Monterey Jack cheese
8 flour tortillas (10 to 12 inches in diameter)
Vegetable oil (see step 3)

1. Combine all the salsa ingredients in a small bowl. Let stand 1 hour. Drain well. Serve at room temperature.

2. Evenly distribute the chicken, cheese, and chiles over 4 tortillas. Cover with the remaining tortillas. Pinch the ends together slightly.

3. In a heavy 8- to 10-inch skillet, heat just enough oil to coat the bottom of the pan and keep the tortillas from sticking. Sauté each until the cheese is melted and the quesadilla is lightly browned on both sides.

4. Cut into pie-shaped wedges and serve immediately, with the salsa. Ideally, cook and serve the quesadillas one at a time.

HERB-ROLLED CHICKEN BREAST SLICES

The special fragrance fresh herbs impart, as well as intensity of color, is essential to the success of this dish. And the pretty pinwheel design created by the herb stuffing adds up to a lovely presentation.

18 servings

4 cups fresh bread crumbs, lightly toasted
½ small onion, minced
1 garlic clove, pressed
1 cup minced fresh herbs, a combination of basil, thyme, rosemary, flat-leaf parsley, sage, and marjoram to taste
5 eggs, lightly beaten
½ teaspoon salt
¼ teaspoon freshly ground black pepper
4 whole chicken breasts (about 1 pound each), skinned, boned, halved, and pounded to ½ inch thick
1 teaspoon vegetable oil
Freshly ground black pepper
Fresh herbs for garnish

1. Preheat the oven to 375° F.

2. In a large bowl, combine the bread crumbs, onion, garlic, minced herbs, eggs, salt, and pepper.

3. Lay the chicken breasts skinned side down on a flat surface and cover them with the bread crumb mixture. Roll the breasts, tucking in the edges. Secure the ends with toothpicks.

4. Lightly oil an ovenproof dish. Place the rolls close together in the dish. Sprinkle lightly with pepper, and cover the rolls with a sheet of parchment paper cut to fit just inside the pan. The paper should rest gently on the rolls.

5. Bake the rolls for 15 minutes, or until firm to the touch. Let cool to room temperature and refrigerate. When cold, remove the toothpicks, cut the rolls at a slight angle into ½-inch-thick slices and arrange on a plate, garnished with sprigs of fresh herbs.

MEDITERRANEAN-STYLE CHICKEN BREAST PHYLLO TART

Though phyllo dough may seem intimidating, with its great golden puffs of paper-thin layers enclosing mixtures of both sweet and savory contents, it is fairly easy to work with. Always keep the sheets covered with a lightly dampened dish towel to keep the dough from drying and cracking, which makes it unusable.

12 servings

2 tablespoons olive oil
1 large onion, diced
3 garlic cloves, chopped
1 small sweet red pepper, seeded and cut into julienne
1 small green pepper, seeded and cut into julienne
1 tablespoon finely crumbled dried oregano
2 pounds fresh pear tomatoes, peeled and sliced
Salt to taste
1 cup sliced fresh mushrooms
3 cups chicken stock (see page 9)
3 whole chicken breasts (about 1 pound each)
2 to 3 tablespoons melted butter

1 1-pound package phyllo dough (24 sheets)
1 cup fine dry bread crumbs
½ pound boiled ham, finely diced
1 avocado, peeled and mashed
1 cup chopped pitted Greek or Niçoise olives
1 teaspoon anchovy paste (optional)
Extra-virgin olive oil

1. In a sauté pan, heat 1½ tablespoons of the oil. Over medium heat, sauté the onion, garlic, peppers, and oregano until tender. Add the tomatoes and salt. Sauté for an additional 5 minutes, then remove to a bowl and set aside.

2. In the same pan, heat the remaining ½ tablespoon oil. Over medium heat, sauté the mushrooms for 2 minutes. Set aside.

3. In a 2-quart saucepan, heat the chicken stock and poach the breasts for 10 minutes. Do not overcook. The breasts will be firm when pressed with a fork. Let the breasts cool in the stock. Remove the skin and bones. Tear the meat into bite-size pieces and set aside.

4. Preheat the oven to 375° F.

5. Lightly brush a metal baking sheet with melted butter. Lay two sheets of phyllo dough on the baking sheet. Brush with melted butter and sprinkle with bread crumbs. Lay two more sheets of phyllo on top and continue in this manner until 12 sheets of phyllo have been used.

6. Sprinkle on the chicken. Layer on the ham, cooked vegetables, avocado, and olives. Dot with anchovy paste (optional).

7. Finish by covering the tart with the remaining phyllo, using melted butter and bread crumbs between each layer. When all the phyllo has been used, slice the tart into 12 pieces, but *do not separate them*. Brush the top with more melted butter and extra-virgin olive oil. Baste several times during baking.

8. Bake for 20 to 30 minutes, or until golden brown.

9. Let the tart cool on a rack. Cut the pieces through. Serve warm or at room temperature.

SHOP UNTIL YOU DROP!

In the old days, going to the supermarket was hardly a glamorous chore. A dutiful once-a-week visit filled the pantry with workaday groceries, toilet paper, detergent, and bleach. Deli sections usually limited their offerings to tired barbecued chickens rotating on a spit and rubbery green gelatin salads. Anything fancier had to be purchased at special markets that catered to the wealthy, whose services included telephone orders, charge accounts, and door-to-door delivery. These food boutiques were probably the only places in town to buy lamb's lettuce, radicchio, and French goat cheese. Now all one has to do is ask at almost any market, "What price pleasure?" These days, even the most ordinary markets have fresh bakeries, coffee bars, antipasto counters, salad bars, sushi chefs, and butchers for custom cutting on the premises. Ranking supreme in the poultry department is the chicken breast, which can be found skin-on bone-in, skin-off bone-in, skin-and-bone-off, halved, or whole; even packages of the tiny, tender fillets are available. Quality comes into play as well, especially when the breasts are from free-range chickens. Of course, the price usually reflects the degree of piking, patting, pounding, and customizing that has been done by the hands of the butcher. Seven years ago, when the first chicken breast cookbook was conceived, breast of chicken was not always available separate from the whole bird.

Consider how much our tastes have changed in these few short years, and how chicken breasts, once thought a luxury by many, have unquestionably become a staple in our kitchens.

CALIFORNIA ROLL

For the ultimate taste without the extra calories, make a California Roll without rice. A dozen of these hand rolls (as they are called at the sushi bar) arranged on a platter make an extraordinary display on a grazing buffet. Serve with a bowl of soy sauce flavored with wasabi.

6 to 8 servings

1 cup chicken stock (see page 9)
16 chicken breast fillets, tendons removed
4 sheets of toasted nori (dried seaweed), approximately 7 by 8 inches
2 cups steamed sushi rice
2 teaspoons powdered wasabi, mixed with 1 teaspoon water
½ avocado, peeled and cut lengthwise into thin strips
2 1-inch pieces of cucumber, peeled, seeded, and cut lengthwise into thin strips
2 teaspoons sesame seeds, toasted

4 ounces gari (pickled ginger)
Japanese soy sauce (Tamari), mixed with 2 teaspoons wasabi powder and 1 teaspoon water

1. In a saucepan, heat the stock. Add the fillets and poach over medium heat until slightly underdone, about 3 minutes. Do not overcook. Remove the fillets, place on a platter to cool and set aside.

2. Lay a sheet of nori, rough side up, long side at the bottom, on a bamboo sushi mat. Dip your finger in cold water and pick up a little of the rice at a time, patting it down in a thin layer on the lower half of the nori, all the way to the right and left edges. Spread a small amount of wasabi paste across the rice. Then arrange a fourth of the avocado and cucumber strips lengthwise down the center of the rice. Sprinkle with ½ teaspoon sesame seeds. Lay 4 fillets end to end across the rice.

3. Starting at the edge closest to you, roll up the nori tightly, pressing down on the mat to shape the roll; leave a 1-inch margin of nori at the far end. Moisten the end flap with a little water to seal. Remove the roll from the mat and cut into 8 slices, about 1 inch thick. Repeat with the remaining sushi ingredients.

4. Serve with gari and soy sauce mixed with wasabi.

Note Toasted nori, sushi rice, powdered wasabi, gari, sushi mats, and Japanese soy sauce are available in Oriental markets or ethnic sections of the supermarket.

CAJUN CHICKEN PIECES WITH APRICOT SAUCE

If it's hot and spicy you want, try this fine old Cajun flavor combination, invented in New Orleans.

8 to 10 servings

Apricot Mustard Sauce
1½ cups apricot preserves or apricot purée
6 tablespoons Creole-style mustard (Dijon may be substituted)
3 tablespoons chicken stock (see page 9)

2 teaspoons ground cayenne pepper
2 teaspoons freshly ground black pepper
1 teaspoon freshly ground white pepper
2 teaspoons finely crumbled dried thyme
1 tablespoon garlic powder
1 teaspoon salt
3 whole chicken breasts (about 1 pound each), boned, skinned, halved, and sliced against the grain into 6 to 8 pieces each (fillets may be substituted)
2 tablespoons (¼ stick) unsalted butter
2 tablespoons vegetable oil

1. Apricot Mustard Sauce: In a small saucepan over low heat, cook the preserves, mustard, and stock, stirring constantly, until the preserves melt. Set aside and let cool to room temperature.

2. In a small bowl, combine the peppers, thyme, garlic powder, and salt. Mix well. Sprinkle the chicken with the spice mixture and let stand for 30 minutes.

3. In a sauté pan or heavy skillet, melt the butter with the oil. Add the chicken and sauté just until done, about 3 minutes. Remove with a slotted spoon and drain briefly on a paper towel. Serve immediately with apricot mustard sauce on the side.

CHICKEN CAKES WITH TOMATO CHILI SAUCE

What a tasty surprise the slightly hot dipping sauce lends to the crispy mini cakes—just the right size for one bite. These can easily be passed on a tray with sauce on the side.

12 servings

4 whole chicken breasts (about 1 pound each), boned and skinned
3 tablespoons unsalted butter
½ cup chopped celery
6 scallions (white part only), chopped
2 cups fine dry bread crumbs
2 eggs, lightly beaten
½ cup heavy cream
2 tablespoons Dijon mustard
¼ cup minced fresh parsley
2 tablespoons minced fresh tarragon, or 2 teaspoons very finely crumbled dried tarragon
Salt and freshly ground black pepper to taste

Tomato Chili Sauce
4 tablespoons (½ stick) unsalted butter
2 shallots, minced
6 ripe tomatoes (about 1½ pounds), peeled, seeded, and chopped
¼ cup dry white wine
¼ cup minced fresh parsley
1 to 3 tablespoons chili sauce (see sidebar for recipe or use bottled)
Salt to taste

Vegetable oil
Fresh tarragon or parsley sprigs for garnish

1. In a food processor fitted with a steel blade, process the chicken breast meat until finely chopped. Set aside.

2. In a sauté pan or heavy skillet over medium-high heat, melt the butter. Sauté the celery and scallions until tender, about 5 minutes. Transfer to a medium bowl. Add the chicken, bread crumbs, eggs, cream, mustard, parsley, tarragon, and salt and pepper. Chill for at least 2 hours or overnight.

3. To make the sauce, melt the butter in a sauté pan over medium heat. Add the shallots and sauté until tender, about 5 minutes. Add the tomatoes and cook 6 minutes more. Mix in the wine and cook until the sauce is thick, about 15 minutes. Add the parsley, chili sauce, and salt. Set aside.

4. Preheat the oven to 400° F.

5. Using about 1 tablespoon of the chicken mixture for each, make patties about ½ inch thick.

6. In a sauté pan or heavy skillet, heat about 2 tablespoons of vegetable oil. Carefully sauté the patties over medium-high heat, a few at a time, turning once, until golden brown, or about 4 minutes. (Add oil as needed between batches.)

7. Transfer the patties to an ovenproof dish and bake until done, about 6 minutes. Drain on a paper towel. Garnish with herb sprigs. Serve the sauce, heated, on the side.

MAKE YOUR OWN CHILI SAUCE

Why buy bottled chili sauce when you can make a superior one in minutes? The difference in flavor will astound you, and it keeps in the freezer almost indefinitely.

Preheat the oven to 400° F. While wearing rubber gloves, seed and stem 8 to 10 dried chiles (about ½ ounce total of either anchos, chipotles, or mulatos, or use a combination). Place the chiles on a baking sheet and bake for 4 minutes. Let cool. Put 2½ cups of water in a saucepan. Add the chiles, ½ cup coarsely chopped onion, and 3 chopped garlic cloves. Bring to a boil, lower the heat, and simmer, covered, for 25 minutes, or until the chiles are very soft. Let cool, then strain the liquid into a bowl. In a food processor fitted with a steel blade, purée the solids with just enough of the reserved liquid to make a thickened sauce. Force the sauce through a fine sieve. Add salt and freshly ground black pepper to taste. Refrigerate, covered, for up to 1 week, or freeze in small amounts.

BREAST OF CHICKEN WITH BLACK OLIVE MOUSSE AND TOMATO CREAM SAUCE

Patrick Healy, the grandson of an illustrious American cooking-school teacher, decided to become a chef while dining at perhaps the most famous restaurant in France, Moulin de Mougins, eating the incredible fare of chef Roger Verge, accompanied by Julia Child, one of the best-known food personalities in the United States. Today, after making all the right moves in the culinary world on two continents, chef Patrick Healy, with his French-born wife, Sofie, run the well-loved country-French restaurant Champagne, in Los Angeles. They invite you to sample one of their specialties in your own kitchen.

12 to 16 servings

½ pound finely chopped chicken breast meat (chop in food processor fitted with a steel blade)
1 egg
1 egg white
¼ cup heavy cream
5 heaping teaspoons chopped pitted Niçoise olives
½ teaspoon salt
¼ teaspoon freshly ground white pepper
4 whole chicken breasts (about 1 pound each), boned, skinned, and halved
4 cups chicken stock (see page 9) or water
½ teaspoon salt

Tomato Cream Sauce
2 tablespoons extra-virgin olive oil
4 very ripe pear tomatoes, peeled, seeded, and cut into large chunks
1 shallot, finely chopped
1 small garlic clove, finely chopped
½ cup dry white wine
2 cups heavy cream

1. In a mixing bowl, mix together the chopped chicken, egg, and egg white. Add the olives and mix again. Add the cream in a slow but steady stream. Mix in the salt and pepper. Cover and refrigerate.

2. With a sharp, pointed knife, make an incision through the thickest end of the breasts.

3. Fill a pastry bag with the mousse and pipe the mixture into the pockets. Roll each breast in plastic wrap to form sausage shapes. Set aside. Remove the plastic wrap.

4. To make the sauce, in a saucepan, heat the oil until hot. Add the tomatoes and cook until most of the liquid has evaporated. Add the shallot and garlic. Cook for about 1 minute more. Add the wine and cook until it has evaporated.

5. Add the cream and cook over medium heat until the sauce is thick and coats the back of a metal spoon. Keep warm over a pan of hot water.

6. In a 2-quart saucepan, bring the stock and salt to a gentle simmer. Poach the chicken breasts. Do not overcook. They will be firm when pressed with the back of a fork. Remove the breasts from the stock and drain.

7. Slice the breasts thinly on an angle. Pour the hot sauce around the sides of the rounds. Serve immediately.

"GRAZING"

The tasters of this world invented grazing. Plates in motion, spoons reaching into a neighboring bisque or mousse are increasingly familiar sights at the table these days—even in the poshest restaurants. The French responded to this plate passing and sampling with a *menu dégustation,* while Californians saw grazing more as a buffet concept, similar to the tapas of Spain.

Grazing is a playground for nibblers, and absolute heaven for the insatiable appetite. Imagine inventive tastes like sautéed shiitake mushrooms, sliced smoked chicken breast (see page 104), aromatic-oil-basted radicchio grilled and dressed with lemon juice and freshly snipped chives. Besides being more interesting, these "little meals" are a boon for savvy dieters, who know that three appetizers or salads often constitute a lighter, healthier meal than an average main course with its side dishes.

When serving mini grazing courses, consider dishes with a variety of tastes, textures, and colors. It is perfectly acceptable to serve Chinese stir fry with a Japanese, Thai, or Italian-inspired dish. Just remember, no dish should overpower another.

CALIFORNIA-STYLE CHICKEN NACHOS

A classic California appetizer, which is rarely seen without an accompanying bottle of Dos Equis Mexican beer. Serve with Salsa (page 14) if you absolutely must.

4 to 6 servings

1 8-ounce bag blue corn tortilla chips
6 ounces fresh goat cheese (chèvre), at room temperature
1 cup grilled chicken breast, cut julienne
1 ripe avocado, peeled, pitted, and chopped
8 oil-packed sun-dried tomatoes, drained and cut julienne
3 tablespoons canned jalapeño chiles, drained and thinly sliced
¼ cup fresh cilantro cut, chiffonade

1. Preheat the oven to 500° F. Separate the corn chips and select 32 whole triangles. Arrange on a large baking sheet.

2. Spread the cheese evenly over each chip. Bake 3 minutes. Transfer the chips to a warmed platter. Top with chicken, avocado, tomatoes, chiles, and cilantro.

Note For a very hot flavor, use 1 or 2 tablespoons finely minced fresh jalapeño or serrano peppers. Be sure to wear rubber gloves when handling hot chile peppers.

Spa Cuisine

Down with calories. Up with flavor.

A spa is a place where everyone willingly submits to a program of exercises and special cuisine—Spa Cuisine. What might be thought of as upgraded diet fare can be defined as follows: dishes prepared with ingredients low in fat, saturated fat, and cholesterol, with low or no added sodium or sugar. They are high in protein, complex carbohydrates, and fiber. Add to this the challenge many home cooks and professional chefs have taken upon themselves, which is to be creative within these constraints, and Spa Cuisine begins to look like some kind of a miracle. The recipes on these pages contain some flavors that might sound unfamiliar, or difficult to predict at first, but each one is a delectable creation. Spa Cuisine is definitely here to say!

BREAST OF CHICKEN WITH PEACH AND PINK PEPPERCORN SAUCE

A splash of peach brandy or other fruit liqueur adds depth to the flavors in this recipe. Use fresh apricots instead of peaches in the sauce for an interesting variation.

4 servings

2 large ripe peaches, blanched, peeled, halved, and pitted
1¾ cups dry white wine (Chardonnay)
1 tablespoon unsalted butter
2 whole chicken breasts (about 1 pound each), skinned and boned, with all traces of fat removed
Salt and freshly ground black pepper to taste
1 teaspoon pink peppercorns
1 tablespoon chopped fresh basil
1 ripe peach, sliced, for garnish
4 fresh basil sprigs for garnish

1. In a blender or food processor fitted with a steel blade, purée the blanched peaches with 1 cup of the wine.

2. Melt the butter in a sauté pan over medium heat. Add the chicken breasts and sauté on both sides just until opaque. Add the salt and pepper, peppercorns, chopped basil, and remaining wine. Lower the heat and simmer for 5 minutes.

3. Stir in the peach purée and simmer for 5 minutes. Do not overcook.

4. Arrange the chicken breasts on individual plates and decorate with the peach slices and basil sprigs. Spoon the sauce over the chicken breasts. Serve immediately.

ROSEMARY CHICKEN ROLLS WITH ORANGE-NUT STUFFING

4 servings

4 tablespoons fine fresh whole wheat
    bread crumbs
1 small onion, finely minced
salt and freshly ground black pepper to
    taste
1 tablespoon finely chopped fresh rose-
    mary
3 tablespoons chopped pecans
1 egg, beaten
2 whole chicken breasts (about 1 pound
    each), boned, skinned, and all traces
    of fat removed, flattened to about
    ½-inch thick and edges evenly
    trimmed
1 cup chicken stock, reduced to ⅔ cup
    (see page 9)
1 cup fresh orange juice, reduced to ⅔
    cup
Fresh rosemary sprigs for garnish

1. In a mixing bowl, combine the bread crumbs, onion, salt, pepper, chopped rosemary, pecans, and egg. Press together to make a paste.

2. Place the chicken breasts on a flat work surface. Spread the paste evenly over the breasts. Roll the breasts, tucking in the edges. Secure the ends with toothpicks.

3. Put the rolls in a sauté pan. Add the stock and juice. Bring to a boil, turn the heat to low, and simmer, covered, for 20 to 25 minutes, or until the chicken is tender. Do not overcook. The rolls will be firm when pressed with the back of a fork.

4. Remove the rolls to a serving platter and cover with aluminum foil to keep warm. Remove the toothpicks.

5. Turn the heat to high and boil the liquid until reduced by half. Spoon the sauce over the chicken rolls. Garnish with rosemary sprigs and serve immediately.

POACHED CHICKEN BREASTS WITH BABY VEGETABLES

Baby vegetables are available in gourmet stores and upscale grocery markets. They usually are more expensive than regular-size vegetables. Or use the smallest of the regular vegetables as an economical substitute.

4 servings

6 baby zucchini
6 baby crookneck yellow squash
¼ pound baby carrots, scraped
¼ pound very tiny pearl onions
⅔ cups fava beans (or other beans)
2 garlic cloves, minced
2 tablespoons snipped chives
2 whole chicken breasts (about 1 pound each), boned, skinned, halved, and all traces of fat removed
1¼ cups chicken stock (see page 9)
1 bunch watercress, washed and stemmed
2 teaspoons pesto sauce; or 2 tablespoons fresh basil and ½ small garlic clove, pressed, mixed with 2 teaspoons extra-virgin olive oil
Salt and freshly ground black pepper to taste

1. Put the zucchini, yellow squash, carrots, onions, and beans in a sauté pan or heavy skillet. Sprinkle on the garlic and chives. Arrange the chicken breasts on top.

2. In a blender or a food processor fitted with a steel blade, combine the stock, watercress, pesto sauce, and salt and pepper. Process until puréed.

3. Pour the sauce over the chicken breasts and vegetables. Simmer, covered, over low heat for 20 to 25 minutes, or until the chicken and vegetables are tender.

4. Arrange on a platter, pour on the sauce, and serve immediately.

ORANGE AND BASIL CHICKEN

4 servings

2 whole chicken breasts (about 1 pound each), skinned, split, and all traces of fat removed

Salt and freshly ground black pepper to taste

1 bunch fresh basil leaves

1 cup fresh orange juice, reduced to ½ cup

1 navel orange, cut into thin rounds, for garnish

Fresh basil or parsley for garnish

1. Preheat the oven to 375° F.

2. Sprinkle the chicken breasts with salt and pepper, and place in a single layer in an oiled ovenproof pan.

3. Put a basil leaf beneath and on top of each breast. Pour on the orange juice.

4. Cut a piece of parchment paper to fit just inside the pan. Lightly oil the paper and place it on the chicken breasts.

5. Bake 8 to 10 minutes. Do not over-cook. The breasts will be firm when pressed with the back of a fork. Let cool to room temperature.

6. Arrange on a platter and decorate with orange rounds and basil leaves.

Q: What is the "fillet" portion of the chicken breast, and how should it be cooked and served?

A: It is the most delicate part of the chicken breast, located on the under-side. Fillets (pronounce the "t") are also now sold separately from the breasts, and are frequently used in fajitas, salads, and starters, the finger-size bites. Each fillet, (meaning "rib-bon" in French) equals one small bite of tender meat, and is also virtually fat-free—perfect diet food.

WHITE CHILI

The Canyon Ranch Spa (located in the Berkshires of Massachusetts and in Tucson, Arizona), a fantastic health and fitness resort, is known for its health regimen as well as its imaginative cuisine. Cooking classes are offered daily in order to send ranch visitors home with all the basics of Spa Cuisine. This unusual one-pot, one-dish delight is quick and delicious. You can go to the Canyon Ranch to sample it, or try it at home, with equally good results.

4 servings

1 pound dried Great Northern beans (white beans)
4 cups chicken stock made with 12 or more peppercorns (see page 9)
2 medium onions, coarsely chopped
3 garlic cloves, finely chopped
1 teaspoon salt
½ cup chopped canned green chiles
2 teaspoons ground cumin
1½ teaspoons crushed dried oregano (use a mortar and pestle)
1 teaspoon ground coriander
⅛ teaspoon ground cloves
¼ teaspoon cayenne pepper, or more to taste

2 cups cooked chicken breast chunks
1 cup grated Monterey Jack cheese

1. Soak the beans overnight. Drain and rinse.

2. Combine the beans, stock, half of the onions, and the garlic and salt in a large heavy saucepan or pot and bring to a boil. Reduce the heat, cover, and simmer for 2 hours, or until the beans are very tender, adding more stock as needed. (More stock should not be needed if you are using a heavy pot.)

3. When the beans are tender, add the remaining onions and the chiles, cumin, oregano, coriander, cloves, and cayenne. Mix well and continue to cook, covered, for 30 minutes.

4. Add the chicken and heat through. Spoon 1 cup of chili into each serving bowl, and top with 2 tablespoons of cheese.

CHICKEN BREASTS SCALOPPINE WITH WILD MUSHROOM SAUCE

Use dried wild mushrooms such as morels, porcini, chanterelles, oyster mushrooms or a combination.

4 servings

1 tablespoon extra-virgin olive oil
1 tablespoon walnut oil
2 whole chicken breasts (about 1 pound each), boned, skinned, and flattened to ½ inch thick
2 tablespoons (¼ stick) unsalted butter
2 ounces fresh shiitake or wild mushrooms, or dried mushrooms rehydrated in 1 cup hot water for 30 minutes
¼ pound fresh mushrooms, cleaned and thinly sliced
4 shallots, finely chopped
2 garlic cloves, finely minced
2 cups chicken stock (see page 9)
1 teaspoon chopped fresh thyme, or ¼ teaspoon dried thyme
¼ teaspoon salt
¼ teaspoon freshly ground black pepper
1 teaspoon arrowroot, mixed with 1 tablespoon chicken stock or water

1. In a sauté pan, heat the oils over medium-high heat. One at a time, add the chicken breasts and sear for 30 seconds on each side. Remove to a platter and set aside.

2. Melt the butter in the same pan. Add the mushrooms, shallots, and garlic. Sauté, stirring frequently, for 5 minutes, or until softened.

3. Turn the heat to medium high and add the stock, thyme, salt, and pepper. Bring to a boil, reduce the heat to medium, and simmer until the liquid is reduced by half. Add the arrowroot mixture, stir to mix thoroughly, and simmer for 1 minute more, or until the sauce is slightly thickened.

4. Return the chicken breasts to the pan just long enough to heat through. Serve immediately.

COLD POACHED CHICKEN BREASTS WITH FRESH PAPAYA CHUTNEY

The papaya chutney can be made up to two days in advance and stored, covered, in the refrigerator.

4 servings

2 cups chicken stock (see page 9)
Pinch of salt
2 whole chicken breasts (about 1 pound each)
1 garlic clove, finely minced
1 1-inch piece of fresh ginger, peeled and grated
1 tablespoon mustard seed
¼ cup dark brown sugar
¼ cup sherry vinegar
1 large papaya (about 1 pound), peeled, halved, seeded, and diced

1. In a 2-quart saucepan, heat the stock and salt. Poach the chicken breasts over medium-low heat for 10 minutes, or just until the pink color is gone throughout. Do not overcook. The breasts will be firm when pressed with the back of a fork. Let cool to room temperature in the stock. Remove the bones and skin and discard. Refrigerate the breasts until well chilled.

2. In a heavy saucepan over medium heat, bring the garlic, ginger, mustard seed, sugar, and vinegar to a full boil. Reduce by half.

3. Add the papaya and cook for about 2 minutes. Quickly remove the papaya with a slotted spoon, drain, and place in a bowl. Reduce the pan juices slightly over high heat and pour over the papaya. Refrigerate for at least 2 hours.

4. Arrange the chilled chicken breasts on individual plates, slice on the diagonal, and serve with the papaya chutney on the side.

SPA-STYLE CHICKEN AND VEGETABLE LASAGNA

Some spas allow no more than 6 ounces of meat, fish, or chicken breast per day. Accompanying this portion is a magnificent array of vegetables that never veers from the Spa Cuisine concept: low in fat, sodium, calories, and sugar; filled with flavor.

6 servings

2 whole chicken breasts (about 1 pound each), boned, skinned, and pounded to ¼ inch thick
8 ounces part-skim ricotta cheese
1 teaspoon chopped fresh oregano
1 tablespoon chopped fresh basil
8 ounces fresh whole wheat lasagna noodles, cooked, drained, and cooled
4 cups tomato sauce (homemade if possible)
1 pound carrots, scraped, thinly sliced on the diagonal, and blanched
1 pound zucchini, peeled and sliced into long, thin strips
12 ounces spinach, stems removed, steamed for 2 minutes and drained
½ cup grated part-skim mozzarella cheese

1. Preheat the oven to 350° F.

2. In a nonstick frying pan or a stove-top grilling pan, quickly sear the chicken for about 1 minute on each side. Set aside.

3. In a small bowl, mix the ricotta, oregano, and basil. Line the bottom of a 9 × 11-inch glass baking dish with a layer of noodles. Top with tomato sauce. Add a layer of carrots, followed by layers of zucchini and spinach. Cover with half of the ricotta mixture, then layer the chicken pieces over the ricotta. Repeat, finishing with a layer of pasta. Cover with aluminum foil and bake for 30 minutes.

4. When the lasagna is nearly finished, heat the remaining tomato sauce over medium heat until bubbling.

5. Remove the lasagna from the oven, discard the foil, and cut into 6 portions. Top with tomato sauce and sprinkle with mozzarella. Return the baking dish to the oven and broil for 1 minute, or until the cheese is melted. Serve immediately.

CREOLE CHICKEN

This dish can be served either hot or at room temperature.

4 servings

2 whole chicken breasts (about 1 pound each), boned, skinned, halved, and all traces of fat removed, flattened to 1 inch thick
Salt and freshly ground black pepper to taste
1 tablespoon olive oil
¾ cup finely chopped onion
¾ cup finely chopped celery
⅔ small green bell pepper, seeded and ribbed, finely chopped
2 large garlic cloves, minced
Pinch of cayenne pepper
¾ cup white wine
2 cups canned tomatoes, drained and coarsely chopped
¼ cup tomato paste
½ to 1 teaspoon Tabasco sauce, or to taste
3 tablespoons chopped fresh parsley
½ teaspoon dried thyme
¼ teaspoon salt

1. Sprinkle the chicken with salt and pepper. Set aside.

2. Heat the oil in a sauté pan over medium-high heat. Add the onion, celery, green pepper, garlic, cayenne, and sauté over medium-high heat, stirring frequently, for 5 minutes, or just until the onion is wilted.

3. Add the chicken, wine, tomatoes, tomato paste, Tabasco, parsley, thyme, and salt. Bring to a boil over medium heat and, with the pan partially covered, cook for 6 to 8 minutes, or just until the chicken is done. Do not overcook. Remove the chicken to a platter and cover with aluminum foil to keep warm.

4. Raise the heat to high and reduce the sauce by a third, stirring frequently. Arrange the chicken on individual plates and spoon on the sauce, or serve at room temperature with the sauce heated and served on the side.

TRI-VINEGAR CHICKEN BREASTS

4 servings

1 jalapeño pepper, seeded, stemmed, and minced (wear rubber gloves)
3 garlic cloves, minced
Juice of 1 lemon
2 large chicken breasts with upper wing and bones attached, skinned and all traces of fat removed
1 cup chicken stock (see page 9)
1 cup white wine
1 tablespoon olive oil
¼ cup red wine vinegar
2 tablespoons finest white wine or Champagne vinegar
2 teaspoons balsamic vinegar
Bouquet garni: 1 sprig fresh rosemary or 1 teaspoon dried rosemary, 1 tablespoon fresh tarragon or 1 teaspoon dried tarragon, and 1 bunch parsley stems, tied in a cheesecloth bag
2 tablespoons minced shallots
2 teaspoons tomato paste

1. Combine the jalapeño, garlic, and lemon juice. Spread over the chicken breasts and marinate, covered with plastic wrap, for 2 hours or more at room temperature.

2. In a saucepan, combine the stock and wine. Over medium-high heat, reduce by half. Set aside.

3. Heat the oil in a nonstick skillet. Add the chicken pieces, skinned side down. Cook over medium heat until the breasts are browned on one side, about 3 minutes. Turn over and cook, covered, for 2 minutes more. Remove the chicken from the pan and set aside.

4. Pour any excess fat out of the pan. Add the vinegars and cook over medium heat, stirring and scraping to loosen any browned bits on the bottom of the pan. Stir in the shallots, bouquet garni, tomato paste, and stock reduction. Raise the heat to high and reduce the liquid slightly.

5. Lower the heat and add the chicken breasts. Cook, partially covered, for about 5 minutes, or until the chicken is done and the sauce is thick. Serve immediately.

Salads

**Whatever you thought about chicken salad
before this moment, forget it!**

Chicken salad has risen in status from a mushy, mayonnaisey mess, set uncreatively in the center of a plate of iceberg lettuce, to a composed plate of intricately arranged ingredients. Salads of poached, grilled, smoked, or baked chicken breasts combined with wild rice, grilled vegetables, baby lettuces, unique and exotic ethnic ingredients, fresh herb vinaigrettes, and even fruits are more in step with today's tastes. Restaurants offer chicken breast salads as basic lunch fare in the guise of sophisticated antipastos, or have adapted many classical approaches to accommodate the breasts of chicken, such as Cobb Salad (see page 41). These dishes could easily fill their own book, with so much emphasis on light eating. The next recipes will certainly bring a new perspective on chicken breast salads into your dining room, backyard, or kitchen.

FOUR OAKS WARM CHICKEN SALAD WITH ORANGE VINAIGRETTE

It is often said that restaurants today are part sustenance and part showmanship, and not always in equal portions. Nowhere is the theater of dining more vibrant than in outdoor cafés. Happily, there is one outdoor spot in Los Angeles that combines a delightful atmosphere with divine fare.

Perched along a narrow residential road that snakes through the jagged canyons of Beverly Hills, this twenty-two-year-old establishment has previously been a train station, a brothel, a speakeasy, a gas station, and a sandwich shop owned by "Ma." The Four Oaks is what energetic, innovative Swiss chef Peter Roelant calls his home away from home. If you can't go there to try his chicken breasts over green beans, artichoke hearts, radicchio, and mâche, drizzled with truffle vinaigrette, try this fantastic recipe from Peter and serve it outside.

4 servings

Vinaigrette
¼ cup white wine vinegar
1 tablespoon chopped shallots
Juice of 1 orange, reduced by half
Juice of 1 lemon
3 tablespoons olive oil
Salt and freshly ground black pepper to
    taste

4 Belgian endives, cut very thin julienne
2 tablespoons lemon juice, in 2 cups cold
    water
Peel of 1 orange, cut julienne for garnish
2 chicken breasts (about 1 pound each),
    boned, skinned, and cut into cubes
4 to 6 cups mâche (lamb's lettuce, field
    salad or bibb lettuce), washed and
    dried
1 small tomato, peeled, seeded, and
    diced (about 3 tablespoons)
1 orange, peeled and cut into small
    cubes for garnish

1. In a small saucepan over medium heat, warm the vinegar with the shallots, juice, and salt and pepper. Continue cooking to infuse for about 10 minutes. Stir in the lemon juice. Slowly whisk in the oil, salt, and pepper. Set aside.

2. Refresh the endive leaves in the lemon juice and water. Spin dry and refrigerate until ready to use.

3. Parboil the orange peel twice in boiling water, changing the water each time. Drain and set aside.

4. In a sauté pan, heat the oil. Sauté the chicken breasts over medium heat for about 2 minutes on each side.

5. Meanwhile, mix the lettuce and endive in a bowl. Pour on some of the vinaigrette to taste and toss to coat well. Divide evenly onto four plates. Sprinkle the chicken and oil delicately over the lettuce.

6. Top with the diced tomato and garnish with the orange peel and orange cubes. Serve at room temperature.

PERFECT POACHED CHICKEN BREASTS

If your intention is to poach a chicken breast, here is a no-fail method, also used in the recipes calling for poached breasts throughout this book. I often poach several at a time and freeze them in plastic bags. This is the perfect diet food, and ideal for a quick-fix dinner. Try poached chicken breasts drizzled with Anchovy Mustard Vinaigrette (page 55).

Poaching liquid: 2 cups (or more)
    chicken stock (see page 9), 1 parsley
    sprig, 1 celery leaf, pinch of salt
2 whole chicken breasts (about 1 pound
    each)

1. In a large saucepan or stockpot, bring the poaching liquid to a boil. Add the chicken breasts, arrange in a single layer, and cover. Lower the heat and simmer for 8 to 10 minutes, or just until the pink is gone throughout. The breasts will be firm when pressed with the back of a fork. Let cool to room temperature in the stock.

2. Remove the skin and bones and shred the chicken breasts into bite-size pieces, or split in half.

Note Other ingredients may be added to the poaching liquid: ½ cup white wine, 2 tablespoons lemon juice, 1 tablespoon dried herbs of choice, several peppercorns or allspice berries.

CHINESE CHICKEN SALAD, SZECHWAN STYLE

Szechwan-style Chinese cooking is noted for its heat. This wonderfully flavored recipe is no exception.

4 servings

2 whole chicken breasts (about 1 pound each)
2 cups leeks (green part only) or scallions
2 slices fresh ginger, peeled and sliced

Sauce
2 tablespoons peanut oil
⅓ cup chopped scallions (white part and a little of the green)
2 teaspoons peeled and minced fresh ginger
1 fresh jalapeño, seeded, veins removed, and finely chopped
½ teaspoon ground Szechwan peppercorns
2 tablespoons soy sauce
1 tablespoon hoisin sauce
2 tablespoons fresh orange juice
1 teaspoon honey
2 garlic cloves, minced
1 to 2 teaspoons chili oil

4 cups shredded Shantung or Napa cabbage

1. Fill a 2-quart saucepan with 3 to 4 cups water. Bring to a boil. Add the chicken breasts, leeks, and ginger. Cover the pan tightly and cook over high heat for 10 minutes.

2. Remove from the heat and let the chicken cool in the liquid for 45 minutes. Place the chicken breasts in a strainer for 2 minutes. Remove the bones and skin and discard. Refrigerate, wrapped in plastic, until well chilled. Shred the meat into coarse pieces. Refrigerate again until ready to assemble.

3. In a small saucepan, mix together the peanut oil, scallions, ginger, jalapeño, and ground peppercorns. Set aside.

4. In a small bowl, combine the soy sauce, hoisin sauce, orange juice, honey, garlic, and chili oil. Set aside.

5. Bring the peanut oil mixture to a boil and cook for 1 minute over medium heat. Add the soy sauce mixture and heat together, but do not continue boiling.

6. Combine the cabbage and chicken. Pour on the sauce, toss gently, and serve on individual plates.

CHICKEN BREAST "COBB" SALAD

The fine food at the Brown Derby in Hollywood gained its own fame. The world's first Cobb salad was created when Derby owner Robert Cobb raided his refrigerator seeking a midnight snack for theater magnate Sid Grauman (the original owner of the Hollywood Boulevard landmark Grauman's Chinese Theatre). Cobb's late-night culinary creation was so tasty he added it to the Derby's menu, where it became an instant star.

4 servings

3 whole chicken breasts (about 1 pound each), skinned and boned
Poaching liquid: 4 cups (or more) chicken stock, 1 celery stalk, 1 parsley sprig, pinch of salt.
¼ pound bacon, cooked crisp, drained, and crumbled
1½ avocados, peeled and diced
1½ large beefsteak tomatoes, diced
½ cup Danish blue cheese (or other imported blue), crumbled

Vinaigrette
¼ cup Champagne vinegar
½ cup corn oil
½ cup extra-virgin olive oil
2 garlic cloves, minced
2 teaspoons oregano
½ teaspoon salt
1 teaspoon freshly ground black pepper
Shredded lettuce

1. Poach the chicken breasts in the poaching liquid for 10 minutes, or just until the pink color is gone throughout. The breasts will be firm when pressed with the back of a fork. Let cool to room temperature in the liquid. Cut the chicken julienne. Cut the julienne strips in half.

2. In a medium bowl, mix the chicken, bacon, avocado, tomato, and cheese. Set aside.

3. In a glass jar with a cover, combine the vinaigrette ingredients in a covered jar; shake to combine. Drizzle the vinaigrette onto the salad mixture half at a time (use less if desired). Gently toss until all the pieces are coated.

4. Serve on shredded lettuce and pass the pepper mill.

DILLED CHICKEN WITH SWEET PEPPERS AND CAPPELLINI SALAD

4 servings

¾ pound dried cappellini
2 whole chicken breasts (about 1 pound each)
Poaching liquid: 2 cups (or more) chicken stock (see page 9), 1 parsley sprig, pinch of salt
¼ cup white wine vinegar
2 tablespoons fresh lemon juice
1 tablespoon dry sherry
1 teaspoon medium sherry
1 teaspoon honey
Salt and freshly ground black pepper to taste
½ cup olive oil
1 large red bell pepper, seeded and cut julienne
1 large yellow bell pepper, seeded and cut julienne
1 large cucumber, peeled, seeded, and sliced into thin rounds
½ cup dill sprigs
5 scallions (green and white part), chopped

1. In a large pot of lightly salted boiling water, cook the pasta *al dente*. Drain, rinse, and set aside to cool.

2. Poach the chicken breasts in the poaching liquid for 10 minutes, or just until the pink color is gone throughout. The breasts will be firm when pressed with the back of a fork. Let cool to room temperature in the liquid, remove and discard the bones and skin, and tear into large pieces.

3. In a small bowl, whisk the vinegar, lemon juice, sherries, honey, and salt and pepper. Add the oil in a thin but steady stream, whisking until the dressing emulsifies.

4. In a large bowl, combine the paste with the chicken, peppers, cucumber, dill, and scallions. Pour on the dressing and toss to combine well. Cover the bowl with plastic wrap and chill at least 1 hour before serving.

MOROCCAN-STYLE CHICKEN BREAST SALAD

6–8 servings

4 whole chicken breasts (about 1 pound each), skinned, boned, and grilled (see page 103 for grilling instructions)
2 green peppers, seeded and cut into ¼-inch strips
2 small red onions, thinly sliced
¼ cup chopped fresh parsley
¼ cup chopped fresh cilantro
2 garlic cloves, finely minced
2 bunches watercress, stems removed

Vinaigrette
¼ cup lemon juice
¼ cup red wine vinegar
1 teaspoon paprika
1 teaspoon ground cumin
¼ teaspoon cayenne pepper
Salt and freshly ground black pepper to taste
1 cup extra-virgin olive oil
12 chopped black olives for garnish

1. Cool the chicken breasts to room temperature. Cut into ¼-inch-wide strips.

2. Combine the chicken, peppers, onions, parsley, cilantro, garlic, and watercress.

3. In a small bowl, combine the lemon juice, vinegar, paprika, cumin, cayenne, and salt and pepper. Whisk in the oil in a thin but steady stream until thick and well mixed.

4. Drizzle the vinaigrette over the chicken mixture, half at a time. Gently toss to mix well (use less if desired). Arrange on individual plates and top with olives.

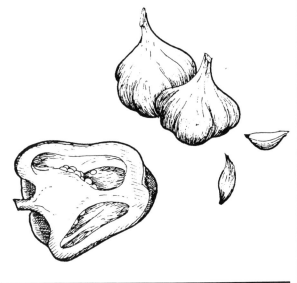

THAI CHICKEN SALAD

Currently, Thai food is the rage. It is an incredibly varied cuisine, with many new and creative ways to prepare chicken breasts, from starters to salads and main courses. Here, two different dressings are provided, each adding a distinctive Thai flavoring. Try them both to find your favorite.

4–6 servings

3 whole chicken breasts (about 1 pound each)

Poaching liquid: 4 cups (or more) chicken stock (see page 9), 2 threads lemongrass, 1 1-inch piece of lime rind, 1 tablespoon fresh lime juice, pinch of salt

5 ounces cellophane noodles (bean threads)

1 cup finely grated carrots

2 cucumbers, peeled, seeded, and chopped

½ cup coarsely chopped roasted peanuts

Dressing

4 large garlic cloves, mashed to a paste with ½ teaspoon salt

¼ cup soy sauce

½ cup fresh lime juice

1 teaspoon grated lime zest

1 tablespoon sugar

1 tablespoon peanut butter

1¼ teaspoons dried hot red pepper flakes

¼ cup sesame oil

1. Poach the chicken breasts in the liquid over medium-low heat for 10 minutes, or just until the pink color is gone throughout. The breasts will be firm when pressed with the back of a fork. Let cool to room temperature in the liquid. Remove and discard the skin and bones. Shred the chicken breasts into bite-size pieces and set aside.

2. Put the noodles in a large ovenproof glass bowl. Pour on boiling water to cover, and let stand for 10 minutes. Drain the noodles and arrange them on a platter or onto individual plates.

3. In a mixing bowl, combine the chicken, carrot, and cucumbers.

4. In a blender, combine the garlic paste, soy sauce, lime juice and zest, sugar, peanut butter, and pepper flakes. With the motor running, add the oil in a thin but steady stream, and blend until very thick.

5. Pour half of the dressing over the chicken mixture and toss to mix well. Arrange the salad in the center of the noodles. Just before serving, top with the peanuts. Serve the remaining dressing on the side.

DRESSING In step 4, combine ¼ cup olive oil, 2 tablespoons hot chili oil, 1 minced large garlic clove, ¼ cup rice wine vinegar, and 3 tablespoons Tamari soy sauce in a small bowl. Add 2 stemmed, seeded, and finely chopped serrano chiles and ¼ cup shredded unsweetened coconut, toasted to light brown. Continue with step 5 as directed.

Note Cellophane noodles and Tamari are available in Oriental markets.

MEXICAN CHICKEN BREAST SALAD

4–6 servings

3 whole chicken breasts (about 1 pound each), skinned and boned
Salt and freshly ground black pepper to taste
¼ cup red wine vinegar
Several dashes of Tabasco sauce
1 16-ounce can chickpeas (garbanzo beans), drained and rinsed
1 red pepper, seeded and diced
1 green bell pepper, seeded and diced
3 celery stalks, diced
1 red onion, finely diced

Dressing
1½ cups sour cream
2 tablespoons chili sauce (bottled, or see page 21)
2 teaspoons ground cumin
2 jalapeño peppers, stemmed, seeded, and finely chopped
1 small bunch cilantro, stems trimmed, finely chopped
Salt and freshly ground black pepper to taste

1. Preheat the oven to 375° F.

2. Place chicken breasts in a lightly oiled baking dish. Sprinkle on salt and pepper and bake for 10 to 12 minutes, or just until done. Do not overcook. Let cool to room temperature. Julienne cut the chicken into ¼-inch strips.

3. In a large bowl, combine the chicken with the vinegar, Tabasco, chickpeas, red and green peppers, celery, and onion. Chill until ready to use.

4. In a bowl, combine the sour cream, chili sauce, cumin, jalapeños, cilantro, and salt and pepper. Mix well.

5. Combine the dressing and the chicken mixture. Mix well and chill 1 hour before serving.

TARRAGON CHICKEN BREAST SALAD WITH TOASTED PECANS

6 servings

3 whole chicken breasts (about 1 pound each)

Poaching liquid: 4 cups (or more) chicken stock (see page 9), 1 celery leaf, 1 parsley sprig, ½ teaspoon dried tarragon, pinch of salt, 2 tablespoons fresh lemon juice

1 cup finely chopped celery hearts

Salt and freshly ground black pepper to taste

⅓ cup lemon mayonnaise (homemade or commercial mayonnaise with 1 tablespoon fresh lemon juice added 24 hours prior to using)

⅓ cup plain yogurt

2 tablespoons tarragon white wine vinegar

1 tablespoon chopped fresh tarragon or 1¼ teaspoons crumbled dried tarragon

1 cup chopped toasted pecans

1. Poach the chicken breasts in the poaching liquid for 10 minutes, or just until the pink color is gone throughout. Do not overcook. The breasts will be firm when pressed with the back of a fork. Let cool to room temperature in the liquid. Remove and discard the skin and bones, and shred the chicken breasts into bite-size pieces. Put in a mixing bowl.

2. Mix in the celery. Sprinkle on the salt and pepper. Set aside.

3. In a small bowl, mix the mayonnaise, yogurt, vinegar, and tarragon. Add the dressing to the chicken and mix well. Chill for 1 hour. Just before serving, stir in the pecans.

ITALIAN CHICKEN AND VEGETABLE SALAD

Serve this nouvelle Italian delight with a glass of dry Pinot Grigio (similar to California Chardonnay). This salad is also recommended for lunch buffets, but not necessarily for picnic fare, as it must remain well chilled before serving (unrefrigerated mayonnaise can go bad in a very short time in hot weather).

4–6 servings

2 whole chicken breasts (about 1 pound each)
Poaching liquid: 2 cups (or more) chicken stock (see page 9), 1 celery leaf, 1 parsley sprig, pinch of salt, 1 tablespoon fresh basil leaves
½ pound rotelle pasta (spinach, tomato, and egg combination)
¾ cup cubed zucchini
¾ cup seeded, peeled, and diced tomatoes
½ cup thinly chopped celery
½ cup sour cream
⅓ cup mayonnaise
1½ teaspoons lemon juice
4½ teaspoons dried basil
1 teaspoon dried oregano
¾ teaspoon salt
⅛ teaspoon black pepper
2 tablespoons chopped fresh parsley for garnish
¼ cup toasted pine nuts

1. Poach the chicken breasts in poaching liquid for 10 minutes, or just until the pink color is gone throughout. The breasts will be firm when pressed with the back of a fork. Let cool to room temperature in the liquid. Remove and discard the skin and bones. Shred the chicken and set aside.

2. In a large pot of lightly salted boiling water, cook the pasta *al dente*. Drain and rinse well with hot water. Let cool.

3. In a large bowl, combine the chicken, pasta, zucchini, tomatoes, and celery.

4. In another bowl, combine the sour cream, mayonnaise, lemon juice, basil, oregano, salt, and pepper. Fold into the chicken mixture, sprinkle on the parsley and pine nuts, and mix again. Chill for 2 hours before serving. Pass the pepper mill when serving.

APPLE AND WALNUT CHICKEN SALAD

Serve this classic fruit and chicken salad on a bed of red and white cabbage. In addition to this, there are several other fruit and chicken breast combinations you might want to fix. See the variations below for inspiration—each one is as easy as this recipe.

4–6 servings

3 whole chicken breasts (about 1 pound each)
Poaching liquid: 4 cups (or more) chicken stock (see page 9), 1 celery leaf, 1 parsley sprig, pinch of salt, 1 tablespoon fresh lemon juice
2 tart green apples, cored, peeled, and cut into ½-inch slices
4 tablespoons fresh lemon juice
⅔ cup chopped pitted dates
1 cup finely chopped celery (use the inner stalks)
⅓ cup sour cream
⅓ cup mayonnaise
Salt and freshly ground white pepper to taste
½ cup chopped toasted walnuts

1. Poach the chicken breasts in the poaching liquid for 10 minutes, or just until the pink color is gone throughout. The breasts will be firm when pressed with the back of a fork. Let cool to room temperature in the liquid. Remove and discard the skin and bones, and shred the chicken into bite-size pieces.

2. In a large bowl, toss the apples with half of the lemon juice. Add the chicken, dates, and celery. Toss to mix well.

3. In a small bowl, whisk together the sour cream, mayonnaise, and remaining lemon juice. Add to the chicken mixture, along with salt and pepper. Toss again to combine well.

4. Cover and chill the salad for 1 hour or more. Just before serving, stir in the walnuts.

RED AND GREEN GRAPES CHICKEN SALAD
Prepare the chicken (step 1) and combine the dressing ingredients (step 3). Toss with the ingredients below.

1 cup each green and red seedless grapes
4 scallions, chopped
Toasted slivered almonds
1 cup chopped celery

MANGO CHICKEN SALAD Follow step 1 as above. Combine the sour cream and mayonnaise with the curry powder and cumin. Continue as directed with the remaining ingredients listed below. Top with chopped cilantro just before serving.

2 mangoes, peeled, pitted, and cut into ¾-inch pieces
½ teaspoon curry powder
¼ teaspoon ground cumin
1 cup coarsely chopped toasted cashews
2 tablespoons chopped cilantro

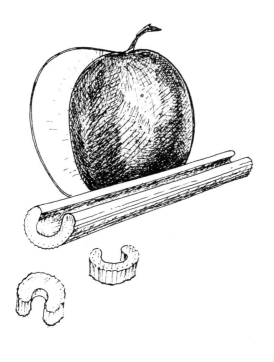

GRAPEFRUIT CHICKEN SALAD Prepare the chicken and sour cream mixture as above. Toss with the ingredients below, adding the nuts just before serving.

1 pink grapefruit, peeled and sectioned
1 Belgian endive
½ cup chopped fresh dill
1 teaspoon fresh lemon juice
1 cup chopped roasted hazelnuts

SUBSTITUTIONS ALLOWED

So you looked the recipe over and several of the required ingredients are not in your cupboard and there's just no way you're going back to the store. What to do? Substitute! Pastas, for instance: use any thin dried or fresh pasta for cappellini in the Dilled Chicken with Sweet Peppers and Cappellini Salad (page 42). Extra-virgin olive oil is not a must; if you don't have any around, use corn oil mixed with any olive oil. Nuts can always be exchanged in recipes. What's more, a creative substitution can often lead to a whole new recipe—so take a chance!

CHICKEN WITH BLACK BEAN SALAD AND CUMIN VINAIGRETTE

6 servings

2 cups black beans, soaked in water for 12 hours or overnight
½ onion, chopped
½ teaspoon salt
3 whole chicken breasts (about 1 pound each), boned and skinned

Vinaigrette
¾ cup extra-virgin olive oil
¼ cup white wine vinegar
1 tablespoon fresh lemon juice
2 teaspoons Dijon mustard
1 tablespoon minced fresh parsley
2 teaspoons ground cumin
½ teaspoon freshly ground black pepper
1½ teaspoons salt

2 large tomatoes, peeled, seeded, and coarsely chopped
½ red bell pepper, seeded and finely chopped
½ green bell pepper, seeded and finely chopped

1. Drain the beans and rinse well. In a medium saucepan, combine the beans, onion, and salt with 6 cups cold water. Bring to a boil. Reduce the heat to low and simmer the beans until tender, about 30 to 40 minutes. Drain and let cool to room temperature.

2. Place the chicken breasts in a shallow glass dish.

3. In a small bowl, whisk together the olive oil, vinegar, lemon juice, mustard, parsley, cumin, pepper, and ½ teaspoon of the salt. Pour two-thirds of the vinaigrette over the chicken breasts. Cover and marinate at room temperature for 30 minutes or more.

4. Prepare the grill (see grilling instructions on page 103) or heat the broiler.

5. Place the beans in a mixing bowl. Add the tomatoes, peppers, and remaining salt and vinaigrette. Toss to combine well and set aside.

6. Cook the chicken breasts 6 to 8 inches from the heat for 4 to 5 minutes on each side, basting once during cooking. Let cool to room temperature.

7. Tear the chicken breasts into bite-size pieces and toss with the beans. Cover and refrigerate until ready to serve.

CHICKEN BREASTS AND BROCCOLI FLORETS WITH TANGY CARROT DRESSING

4 servings

2 whole chicken breasts (about 1 pound each)
Poaching liquid: 2 cups (or more) chicken stock (see page 9), 1 parsley sprig, pinch of salt
2 cups broccoli florets or mixed broccoli and cauliflower florets
1 sweet red pepper, seeded and chopped

Dressing
6 to 8 carrots (about ½ pound), peeled and thinly sliced
4 garlic cloves, minced
1 teaspoon chopped fresh thyme, or ¼ teaspoon dried thyme
2 tablespoons chopped fresh basil, or 1 teaspoon dried basil
1 cup chicken stock
¼ cup tarragon vinegar
1 tablespoon olive oil
¼ teaspoon salt
Pinch of freshly ground white pepper

1. Poach the chicken breasts in the poaching liquid for 10 minutes, or just until the pink color is gone throughout. The breasts will be firm when pressed with the back of a fork. Let cool to room temperature in the stock. Remove and discard the skin and bones, and shred the chicken into bite-size pieces.

2. In a large mixing bowl, combine the broccoli florets, red pepper, and chicken. Chill, covered, until ready to use.

3. In a saucepan, combine the carrots, garlic, thyme, basil, and stock. Bring to a boil over medium heat, stirring occasionally. Lower the heat and simmer, uncovered, for 15 minutes, or until the carrots are very tender. Let cool slightly. Put the mixture in a blender or a food processor fitted with a steel blade. Add the vinegar, oil, salt, and pepper. Purée until smooth.

4. Pour the dressing over the chicken mixture and combine well. Refrigerate at least 2 hours before serving.

CHICKEN SALAD AND GRILLED VEGETABLES WITH THYME VINAIGRETTE

When the coals are hot, throw anything you like around the outer rim of the grill. Wrap a whole head of garlic, drizzled with some olive oil, in aluminum foil and grill for 1 hour. Just before it's ready, grill some thick slices of French bread to spread the baked garlic on. It's a delicious appetizer while the chicken breasts sizzle.

4–6 servings

3 whole chicken breasts (about 1 pound each), skinned and boned
Vegetable oil
Salt and freshly ground black pepper
4 ears of corn, shucked and cooked
2 large zucchini, scrubbed, blanched in boiling water for 3 minutes, and quartered lengthwise
¾ cup finely chopped red onion, soaked in ice water for 10 minutes, drained, and patted dry
2 red bell peppers, seeded and quartered
6 to 8 scallions

Vinaigrette
2 tablespoons white wine vinegar
2 teaspoons grainy mustard
1 garlic clove, minced
1 tablespoon minced fresh thyme, or 1 teaspoon dried thyme
Salt and freshly ground black pepper to taste
3 tablespoons olive oil
3 tablespoons vegetable oil
3 tablespoons chopped fresh cilantro or parsley for garnish

1. Prepare a charcoal fire (see page 103 for grilling instructions). Brush the chicken breasts with oil and season with salt and pepper. When the coals are hot with a layer of white ash, grill the chicken breasts 6 to 8 inches away from the heat for 5 minutes per side. Do not overcook.

2. Transfer the grilled breasts to a cutting board and let cool to room temperature. Slice into ⅓-inch-wide lengthwise strips.

3. Brush the corn with oil and place on the grill toward the outer rim, away from the intense heat source, for about

10 minutes. Turn occasionally until it is lightly colored and grill marks appear. Grill the zucchini, onion, bell peppers, and scallions in the same manner. Exact grilling time will be different for each vegetable. They are done when tender but not soft.

4. In a small bowl, combine the vinegar, mustard, garlic, thyme, and salt and pepper. Whisk in the oils in a thin, steady stream until well combined.

5. Arrange the chicken strips and vegetables on individual plates or one large

platter. Drizzle on half of the vinaigrette and pass the rest on the side. Sprinkle with cilantro. Serve at room temperature.

Note In the event that the grill is too much trouble, don't fret. Grilled food can be made in a well-seasoned ridged cast-iron grill pan, over moderately high heat on the stove. Of course, the overall taste will lack the flavor only burning wood and coals can provide, but the look will be similar.

Q: How do you adjust the heat of a chile pepper?

A: The small, hotter peppers are named serranos. Jalapeños are not as hot. If you want a dish to be generally flavored by the chile pepper but not a tongue burner, use the larger peppers with the seeds and veins removed, (or) a small amount of the hot jalapeños, very finely minced. Always wear rubber gloves while handling peppers and wash your hands after to remove the hot chili oils. (Be careful not to touch your face before washing your hands.) Wash work surfaces and knives as well.

CHICKEN BREAST AND ASPARAGUS SALAD WITH HAZELNUT BALSAMIC VINAIGRETTE

Chicken breasts conveniently become tasty envelopes for almost any type of stuffing. Since the pocket is small, stuffings with intense flavorings are best.

4–6 servings

3 whole chicken breasts (about 1 pound each), skinned, boned, and halved
⅓ cup white wine vinegar
⅛ cup extra-virgin olive oil
1 small onion, sliced into rounds
1 garlic clove, minced
2 tablespoons chopped fresh parsley
Salt and freshly ground black pepper to taste
10 skinny asparagus spears, tough ends trimmed
1 cup chicken stock, reduced to ¼ cup (see page 9)
2 heads bibb lettuce, washed and spun-dried

Vinaigrette
2 tablespoons balsamic vinegar
⅓ cup extra-virgin olive oil
1 teaspoon minced shallots
¼ teaspoon Dijon mustard
¼ teaspoon honey

¼ cup very finely chopped toasted hazelnuts (use a blender or nut chopper)
2 tablespoons coarsely chopped toasted hazelnuts for garnish
8 or more cherry tomatoes, halved

1. To create a pocket for the stuffing, make an opening along the side of each breast, using a sharp knife. Place the breasts in a shallow glass dish.

2. In a small bowl, whisk together the vinegar, oil, onion, garlic, and parsley. Season with salt and pepper. Pour over the breasts, cover with plastic wrap, and refrigerate at least 2 hours.

3. Preheat the broiler.

4. To cook the asparagus, bring a medium pot of water to a rolling boil. Drop in the asparagus and blanch for a minute or two, or until tender but still firm. Drain and let cool. Cut into 2-inch pieces, reserving the tips.

5. Remove the onion from the marinade and finely dice. In a small bowl, combine 2 tablespoons of the stock and the onions. Divide the mixture evenly between the breasts and stuff into the pockets.

Arrange the breasts on a baking sheet covered with aluminum foil. Broil 4 to 5 minutes per side. Let cool slightly.

6. While the breasts are cooking, tear the lettuce into pieces. Arrange in a salad bowl along with the asparagus pieces.

7. In a small bowl, whisk together the vinegar, oil, stock, shallots, mustard, honey, and finely chopped hazelnuts. Mix well.

8. Pour the vinaigrette into a small saucepan. Briefly heat just until warm. Immediately drizzle over the lettuce and asparagus tips, and toss to coat well. Arrange on a platter and place the chicken breasts in the center of the salad. Sprinkle the coarsely chopped hazelnuts on top. Arrange the asparagus tips and cherry tomatoes around the side. Pass the remaining dressing separately.

DRESSINGS AND VINAIGRETTES

Create a quick meal with your favorite greens and salad fixings and, of course, a piece of grilled or poached chicken breasts. These dressings can also be used as marinades for chicken breasts before baking, broiling, or grilling.

Sesame Ginger Dressing
4 garlic cloves, minced
2 tablespoons minced fresh ginger
1 cup Oriental sesame paste
5 tablespoons soy sauce
1 tablespoon sugar
1 tablespoon hot chili oil
3 tablespoons dark Oriental sesame oil
3 tablespoons white wine or dry
    vermouth
6 scallions, sliced
6 tablespoons chopped cilantro

Anchovy Mustard Vinaigrette
1½ tablespoons Dijon mustard
1 2-ounce can anchovies, drained and
    minced
¼ cup red wine vinegar
⅔ cup olive oil
2 scallions, minced
1½ teaspoons crumbled dried thyme
Freshly ground black pepper to taste

Raspberry Walnut Vinaigrette
½ cup plus 2 tablespoons raspberry
    vinegar
½ cup extra-virgin olive oil
2 tablespoons walnut oil
1 garlic clove, minced
2 tablespoons chopped fresh parsley
⅓ cup finely minced shallots

1. To make the dressings, combine all the ingredients in a glass jar with a cover.

2. Shake well and pour over the salad.

BRAZILIAN CHICKEN BREAST SALAD

4 servings

Salt and freshly ground black pepper
2 whole chicken breasts (about 1 pound
  each), skinned and boned
2 green bell peppers, seeded and cut
  julienne
1 sweet red pepper, seeded and cut
  julienne
4 hearts of palm, cut into ¼-inch slices
1 banana, peeled and cut into ¼-inch
  slices

Dressing
6 tablespoons olive oil
⅓ cup orange juice
2 tablespoons lime juice
4 tablespoons red wine vinegar
1 teaspoon crushed dried chiles
Pinch of cayenne pepper
1 teaspoon Tabasco sauce
Pinch of sugar
Pinch of salt

1. Preheat the oven to 375° F.

2. Sprinkle salt and pepper on the chicken breasts. Bake 10 to 12 minutes, or just until done. Do not overcook. Let cool to room temperature and cut julienne.

3. In a mixing bowl, combine the chicken, peppers, hearts of palm, and banana. Toss gently. Sprinkle with salt and pepper.

4. In a blender, combine the oil, juices, vinegar, chiles, cayenne, Tabasco, sugar and salt. Blend well. Add the dressing to the chicken mixture, half at a time, and toss to coat well (use less if desired). Chill before serving.

CHICKEN AND TOFU SALAD WITH TARRAGON WILD RICE

4 servings

1 cup raw wild rice
4 cups chicken stock (see page 9)
2 teaspoons chopped fresh tarragon, or
     1 teaspoon dried tarragon
1 garlic clove, unpeeled
Pinch of salt
1 tablespoon safflower oil
4 slices tofu (approximately ½ inch
     thick), diced

Vinaigrette
2 tablespoons extra-virgin olive oil
2 tablespoons rice wine vinegar
2 tablespoons fresh lime juice
1 tablespoon grainy mustard
2 tablespoons minced shallots
1 tablespoon chopped fresh chives
Pinch of salt
⅛ teaspoon freshly ground white pepper
20 Belgian endive spears
2 large carrots, shredded
2 large zucchini, shredded
10 cherry tomatoes, halved for garnish

2 cups shredded poached chicken breasts
     (see page 39)
¼ cup chopped fresh chives
3 tablespoons chopped Italian flat-leaf
     parsley
1 small red onion, minced
½ green bell pepper, seeded and minced

1. Put the wild rice in a bowl, cover with hot tap water, and soak for 30 minutes. Drain.

2. Put the stock, tarragon, garlic, and salt in a 5-quart saucepan. Bring to a boil, add the wild rice, stir once, and simmer over very low heat for 45 minutes. Remove from the heat and let stand, covered, for 15 minutes. Drain thoroughly. Remove the garlic, fluff the rice, and put it in a bowl to cool. Set aside.

3. In a sauté pan, heat the safflower oil. Sauté the tofu over medium-high heat until lightly browned and slightly crispy. Set aside.

4. In a small bowl, combine the ingredients. Whisk to mix well.

5. Add the chicken, chives, parsley, onion, and green pepper to the wild rice. Drizzle on the dressing and toss gently until well combined. Let stand at room temperature for 2 hours.

6. On individual plates, arrange the endive spears with mounds of shredded carrots and zucchini in the center. Place scoops of the chicken and rice mixture in the center of the plate. Decorate with the cherry tomatoes around the salad.

Sautéing

A splash of this. A dash of that.

Sautéing is just like pan broiling, except that just a little fat is added to the pan first. The basics are simple: Heat a tablespoon or two of butter or oil, or combination of the two, in a heavy skillet or sauté pan over medium-high heat. (Oil lets the butter come to a higher temperature without burning.) Pat the chicken breasts dry and place in the skillet. Cook without moving the pieces until the underside is brown. Turn and sauté the other side. Don't crowd the pan or the pieces will steam and never develop a golden crisp crust.

A companion technique to sautéing is deglazing, which can create an instant, flavorful sauce. Start by removing the chicken breasts from the pan to a platter.

Cover with foil to keep the chicken warm. Quickly add a small amount (¼ to ½ cup) of stock or wine to the pan. Turn the heat to medium high, scraping loose any browned particles stuck to the bottom of the pan. Bring the liquid to a boil and cook, stirring, until reduced. It will be fairly thin, since there is no thickener added to this simple type of sauce. A splash of liquor, such as brandy, port, Grand Marnier, or vermouth, along with a few tablespoons of chopped fresh herbs, can be added along the way to ensure a flavorful sauce. Taste and adjust the seasoning with salt and freshly ground pepper. That's all there is to creating the perfect sauté!

SAUTEED BREAST OF CHICKEN WITH FOIE GRAS AND TRUFFLE SAUCE

A festive and fancy recipe from chef Joe Miller.

Chicken breasts no longer need be ignored during the holidays. Make this wonderful dish especially during the winter months, from December to February, when truffles are in season and foie gras is plentiful. That's when this dish appears on the menu of the Brentwood Bar and Grill, the closest you'll get to New York dining in Los Angeles. This contemporary grill, with Joe Miller presiding over the glass-enclosed kitchen, offers cuisine with French and Italian influences, prepared by an amazing American chef.

4 servings

½ ounce fresh black truffles (or canned if necessary), finely diced
¼ cup olive oil
¼ cup Madeira
1 cup chicken stock (see page 9)
¾ cup heavy cream
2 whole chicken breasts (about 1 pound each), boned, skinned (at least 8–10 ounces), and split
4 ounces fresh duck foie gras
2 large eggs, lightly beaten
½ cup fine fresh bread crumbs

1. Sauté the truffles briefly in 2 tablespoons of the oil. Deglaze the pan with Madeira and reduce by half over medium-high heat. Add ¾ cup of the stock and reduce by half again. Add the cream and again reduce, until the mixture is a saucy consistency. Set aside.

2. Preheat the oven to 400° F. Make an incision in the thickest part of the breast on the underside. Insert even amounts of foie gras in the four breast pieces. Press the breasts closed. Dip the breasts into beaten egg, then coat with bread crumbs.

3. Heat about 2 tablespoons of the remaining oil in a heavy sauté pan over medium heat. Add the chicken breast pieces and sauté until browned on one side. Do not crowd the pan. Turn and brown on the other side, using more oil as necessary. (The chicken should be crispy and brown, the bread crumbs forming a shell.) Place the chicken in the oven for 5 minutes to finish cooking.

4. Reheat the sauce over low heat.

5. Place the chicken on individ heated plates. Pour the sauce a sides of the chicken. Serve immedia

CHICKEN BREASTS WITH BASIL WINE SAUCE

Simple and quick—you can whip this one up in a minute with ingredients from the fridge. And it's sophisticated enough to serve on the most elegant occasions, without a lot of calories!

4 servings

2 tablespoons (¼ stick) unsalted butter
2 whole chicken breasts (about 1 pound each), skinned, boned, halved, and flattened slightly
2 shallots, minced
2 cloves garlic, minced
1 cup dry white wine
½ cup light cream
2 cups chopped fresh basil (do not pack tightly)
3 tablespoons chopped fresh parsley
Salt and freshly ground black pepper to taste

1. Preheat the oven to 275° F.

2. In a sauté pan, melt the butter. Sauté the chicken breasts over medium-high heat about 3 minutes on each side. When almost done, remove to a platter and place in the oven.

3. Reduce the heat to low and add the shallots and garlic to the pan. Sauté until the shallots are soft but not brown, about 5 minutes.

4. Increase the heat and deglaze the pan with the wine and cream. Cook 3 minutes more to reduce slightly. Add the basil, parsley, and season with salt and pepper, and return the chicken breasts to the pan. Quickly heat through, and serve immediately.

BREAST OF CHICKEN WITH PASSION FRUIT BUTTER

Chef John Sedlar of Saint Es-tèphe says some of California Cooking's newest ingredients come from the Caribbean and Latin America. One is passion fruit. "Its sprightly tart-sweet flavor is very fresh and very '90s. To me, passion fruit seeds look like black caviar, and as a garnish they give a touch of ele-gance."

6 servings

Passion Fruit Butter
1 cup dry white wine
1 teaspoon red wine vinegar
1 medium shallot, finely chopped
½ cup heavy cream
1½ cups (3 sticks) cold unsalted butter, cut into small pieces
9 passion fruits, halved, seeded, and pulp scooped out and reserved

6 8–10-ounce boneless chicken breasts, first joint of the wing bones attached
1 teaspoon salt
1 teaspoon freshly ground white pepper
2 tablespoons vegetable oil
2 passion fruits, halved, seeds and pulp scooped out and reserved, for gar-nish

1. Preheat the oven to 375° F.

2. In a medium saucepan over moderate to high heat, boil the wine, vinegar, and shallot until the liquid is reduced by half, about 10 minutes. Add the cream and continue boiling until reduced to ½ cup. Set aside.

3. While the sauce is reducing, season the chicken breasts with salt and pepper and brush with oil. Place on a baking sheet and bake for about 17 minutes, or until lightly golden.

4. After the sauce has reduced, whisk in the butter pieces, one at a time, then whisk in the passion fruit pulp. Strain the sauce through a fine sieve, and re-turn to the pan to keep warm.

5. Slice each chicken breast at a 45-degree angle into ¼-inch-thick pieces. Fan the pieces of each breast across a warmed plate. Spoon the sauce over the chicken, and garnish with a sprinkling of the additional passion fruit pulp and seeds. Serve immediately.

SAUTEED CHICKEN IN COINTREAU

Chicken breasts classically pair up with oranges and other citrus fruit. In this recipe, a splash of that divine French orange liqueur Cointreau deepens and enriches the orange experience.

4 servings

2 whole chicken breasts (about 1 pound each), skinned, boned, and evenly pounded to ½ inch thick
Salt and freshly ground white pepper to taste
2 eggs, lightly beaten
All-purpose flour for dredging
7 tablespoons unsalted butter
2 tablespoons chopped shallots
¾ cup Chardonnay or other good dry white wine
½ cup fresh orange juice, reduced to ¼ cup
⅓ cup Cointreau
1 tablespoon Dijon mustard
1 teaspoon all-purpose flour
1 orange, thinly sliced, for garnish

1. Preheat the oven to 275° F.

2. Sprinkle the chicken with salt and pepper. Put the eggs and flour in separate shallow bowls. Dip each breast in the eggs, then in the flour. Shake off any excess flour.

3. In a sauté pan, melt 3 tablespoons of butter. Sauté the chicken over medium-high heat until golden brown on both sides, about 4 minutes. Transfer to a platter and place in a warm oven.

4. Pour all but 1 tablespoon fat from the sauté pan. Add the shallots and sauté until softened but not browned, about 1 minute. Set aside.

5. In a saucepan over high heat, reduce the wine, juice, and Cointreau by half. Whisk in the mustard and shallots and the remaining butter. Continue whisking until the butter is melted. Add the flour and stir until the sauce comes to a boil. Place the chicken breasts on individual plates, spoon on the sauce, garnish with orange slices, and serve immediately.

Q: What does the word *volaille* have to do with chicken breasts?

A: That's how you say chicken breast in French!

CHICKEN WITH SOUR CHERRIES

If you would prefer another fruit, blackberries or raspberries may be substituted. Choose a corresponding liqueur.

4 servings

2 tablespoons (¼ stick) unsalted butter
1 tablespoon olive oil
2 whole chicken breasts (about 1 pound each), skinned, boned, and pounded to ⅓ inch thick
1 large shallot, finely minced
¼ cup fruit-scented vinegar (sour cherry if possible)
¼ cup chicken stock (see page 9)
¼ cup crème fraîche or heavy cream
1 tablespoon cherry liqueur or brandy
16 whole sour cherries, pitted
Italian flat-leaf parsley for garnish

1. In a large sauté pan, heat the butter and oil. Sauté the chicken breasts over medium-high heat until lightly browned, about 3 minutes on each side. Remove from the pan and set aside.

2. Turn the heat to low and add the shallot to the pan. Cook until tender, about 3 minutes.

3. Add the vinegar and cook over high heat until reduced to about 2 tablespoons. Add the stock, crème fraîche, and liqueur and simmer for a minute more, stirring occasionally.

4. Return the breasts and any juices collected on the plate to the pan and cook for about 5 minutes, or until done. Do not overcook.

5. Remove the breasts from the pan and place on a platter. Cover to keep warm. Turn the heat to medium low. Reduce the liquid until it thickens slightly. Add the cherries and cook 1 minute more. Spoon sauce over each serving. Decorate the plate with parsley leaves.

FRENCH MEETS SOUTHWEST COOKING

Much of what is new in California cooking was first introduced at Saint Estèphe, one of the country's most interesting and innovative restaurants. Chef and co-owner John Sedlar has applied his classical French training to the preparation of a Southwestern cuisine that is as gorgeous to look at as it is to eat. Blue corn may fast be becoming ubiquitous, but it was Sedlar who first brought it from New Mexico to Southern California. While Sedlar does seek out the completely new (he is an avid gardener, who experiments with purple beans and hot "inside-out" radishes), most of his "new" discoveries go as far back as the ancient Mayans and Aztecs. In a couple of years we may all be eating black corn, which Sedlar rediscovered when studying Aztec food from a thousand years ago. His first crop is soon to be harvested.

LEMON CHICKEN PAILLARDS

The thinly pounded chicken breast pieces called for in this recipe cook very quickly, so be ready to serve the dish before the cooking begins. Delicate and tender when properly cooked, it also makes a wonderful starter or appetizer.

4–6 servings

3 whole chicken breasts (about 1 pound each), boned, skinned, halved, and flattened to ¼ inch thickness between plastic wrap
Salt and finely ground white pepper to taste
Zest and juice of 3 lemons
1 cup Chardonnay or other good dry white wine
2 garlic cloves, finely minced
½ cup finely chopped shallots
1 teaspoon finely chopped fresh rosemary, or ¼ teaspoon dried rosemary
2 tablespoons chopped fresh oregano, or 1 teaspoon dried oregano
2 tablespoons olive oil
1 teaspoon arrowroot, mixed with 2 tablespoons cold water

1. Place the chicken breasts in a shallow glass dish. Lightly sprinkle with salt and pepper.

2. In a small bowl, combine the lemon zest and juice, wine, garlic, shallots, rosemary, and oregano. Pour over the chicken breasts and coat well. Marinate, covered, for 2 hours at room temperature or 4 hours in the refrigerator.

3. Preheat the oven to 275° F. Drain the chicken, reserving the marinade, and pat dry with paper towels. In a sauté pan, heat the oil. Sauté the chicken breasts over high heat for 3 minutes on each side or just until done. Remove to a platter and place in a warmed oven.

4. To the sauté pan, add the marinade and cook over high heat until reduced by half. Stir in the arrowroot mixture and stir constantly until the sauce thickens slightly.

5. Place the chicken breasts in the sauce and heat through. Serve immediately with the remaining sauce on the side.

SOUTHWESTERN SPICY SAUTEED CHICKEN BREASTS

If you have a taste for the hot and spicy, this is a good recipe to choose.

4 servings

2 tablespoons vegetable oil
8 garlic cloves, thinly sliced
1 to 1½ jalapeño or serrano chilies, stemmed and ribs removed, very finely minced
3 red bell peppers, stemmed, seeded, and finely chopped
2 whole chicken breasts (about 1 pound each), boned, skinned, and lightly pounded to 1 inch thickness between plastic wrap
1 teaspoon paprika
2 teaspoons chili powder
1 tablespoon lime juice
2 cups Chardonnay or other good dry white wine
½ cup finely chopped fresh cilantro
Pinch of cayenne pepper
¼ teaspoon salt

1. Preheat the oven to 275° F.

2. In a sauté pan, heat the oil over medium heat. Add the garlic and peppers and sauté for 5 minutes, stirring frequently.

3. Add the chicken to the pan. Sprinkle on the paprika and chili powder. Add the lime juice and wine and bring to a boil over high heat. Reduce the heat to low, cover the pan, and simmer 6 to 8 minutes, or just until done. Remove the chicken breasts to a platter and place in a warm oven.

4. Over high heat, reduce the sauce by about a fourth, stirring frequently. Stir in the cilantro, cayenne, and salt. Place the chicken breasts on individual plates and spoon on the sauce. Serve immediately.

SAUTEED CHICKEN BREASTS WITH CITRUS BUTTER

A light and airy sauce with the tang of lime or lemon is quick to fix once you know the system for making the delicate beurre blanc sauce. Simply, cold butter is whisked into a reduction of rich and flavorful ingredients in order to make a foamy, intense sauce that must be served immediately.

4 servings

2 whole chicken breasts (about 1 pound each), boned, skinned, halved, and lightly pounded to ¼ inch thickness between plastic wrap
Salt and freshly ground black pepper to taste
2 tablespoons olive oil
8 tablespoons (1 stick) cold unsalted butter, cut into 16 pieces
8 shallots, peeled and finely diced
Juice of 1½ limes or lemons
¼ cup chicken stock (see page 9)
¼ cup dry white wine
½ teaspoon salt
½ teaspoon freshly ground white pepper
1 teaspoon chopped fresh parsley
4 parsley sprigs for garnish

1. Sprinkle the chicken breasts with salt and black pepper.

2. In a sauté pan, heat the oil. Sauté the chicken breasts over high heat for about 1 minute per side. Immediately remove them to a warmed platter, cover with aluminum foil, and set aside.

3. In a medium sauté pan, melt 6 pieces of the butter. Sauté the shallots over medium-high heat until soft, about 2 minutes. Add the juice, stock, and wine. Bring to a boil and reduce by half. Reduce the heat to very low and whisk in the remaining butter, a piece at a time, until smooth and foamy. Remove from the heat. Stir in the ½ teaspoon salt, white pepper, and chopped parsley.

4. Place the chicken breast pieces on individual plates and spoon on the sauce. Decorate the plates with parsley and serve immediately.

SAUTEED CHICKEN BREASTS WITH BUTTERY BROWN SAUCE AND SAGE LEAVES

If you believe in the old adage "The way to a man's heart is through his stomach," then this is the recipe you've been looking for. Just ask Randall Wreghitt, who, after eating it, fell in love—with my cooking.

4 servings

2 whole chicken breasts (about 1 pound each), skinned, boned, and pounded to ½ inch thick
Salt and freshly ground black pepper to taste
2 tablespoons (¼ stick) unsalted butter
8 whole fresh sage leaves
4 tablespoons (½ stick) unsalted butter, melted
3 tablespoons all-purpose flour
1 cup chicken stock (see page 9)
1 cup milk
Dash of cayenne pepper
¼ cup freshly grated Parmesan cheese

1. Sprinkle the chicken breasts with salt and pepper.

2. In a sauté pan, melt the 2 tablespoons butter. Sauté the sage leaves over medium heat for about 30 seconds. Remove and reserve.

3. Add the chicken breasts to the pan and sauté on each side about 3 minutes, or until done. Remove to a platter and cover to keep warm.

4. In a heavy saucepan over medium heat, whisk together the melted butter and flour to make a roux. Cook, whisking frequently, for 5 minutes.

5. In a saucepan, bring the stock and milk to a full boil. Slowly pour the boiling liquid into the roux, whisking vigorously until completely smooth. Reduce the heat and simmer over low heat for 5 minutes, stirring occasionally.

6. Season with salt and pepper. Add the cayenne and stir in the cheese. Simmer 2 minutes more. Place some sauce on a serving platter. Arrange the chicken breasts on the platter. Place the reserved sage leaves on top, and pass the remaining sauce on the side.

THAI CURRY CHICKEN

4 servings

Sauce

2 tablespoons corn oil
1 cup chopped onions
2 ½-ounce packages Thai green curry
 paste
2 tablespoons curry powder (Madras if
 possible)
½ teaspoon ground cardamom
3 teaspoons minced garlic
2 teaspoons minced fresh ginger
1 teaspoon salt
1 pound ripe tomatoes, peeled, cored,
 and seeded, cut into ½-inch cubes
 (about 2½ cups)
Fresh ripe papaya, peeled and cut into
 ½-inch cubes (about 1½ cups)

2 tablespoons corn oil
1 whole chicken breast (about 1 pound),
 boned, skinned, and cut across the
 grain into ½-inch-wide strips
¼-inch-wide strips of 1 red bell pepper,
 blanched
1 cup broccoli florets, blanched
2 tablespoons fresh lime juice
¼ pound snow pea pods, blanched
Salt and freshly ground black pepper to
 taste
1 cup plain yogurt
1 tablespoon finely chopped fresh mint

1. To make the sauce, in a sauté pan, heat the oil. Sauté the onions over medium heat for 5 minutes. Add the curry paste and powder, cardamom, garlic, ginger, and salt, stirring to break up the curry paste. Cook over medium heat for 2 to 3 minutes more. Turn the heat to high, add the tomatoes and papaya, and cook for 5 to 7 minutes. Set aside and keep warm.

2. In a sauté pan, heat the oil. Sauté the chicken breast over medium heat for 5 minutes. Add the red peppers and sauté 2 minutes more. Set the pan aside.

3. Add the broccoli and lime juice to the sauce and heat through. Add the snow peas to the chicken and heat together for 30 seconds.

4. Combine the sauce with the chicken. Season with salt and pepper.

5. Combine the yogurt and mint. Serve the yogurt sauce on the side.

NORTH AFRICAN–STYLE SPICY CHICKEN BREASTS

Serve this dish with couscous. Add currants or raisins to the mix, along with a pinch of allspice, and your average Morrocan meal is ready. Couscous, a grain, is available in most markets in a box and takes only a few minutes to prepare.

6 servings

3 tablespoons olive oil
3 whole chicken breasts (about 1 pound each), skinned and boned
Salt and freshly ground black pepper to taste
1 large onion, chopped
2 teaspoons paprika
1 teaspoon ground ginger
¼ teaspoon turmeric
⅛ teaspoon ground cinnamon
2 tablespoons fresh lemon juice
1 cup chicken stock (see page 9)
1 pound carrots, peeled and cut on the diagonal into ½-inch slices
1 lemon, cut into 8 wedges and seeded

1. In a sauté pan, heat the oil. Sprinkle the chicken breasts with salt and pepper. Sauté over medium-high heat until brown, about 4 minutes on each side. Transfer the breasts to a platter and set aside.

2. Add the onion to the sauté pan. Reduce the heat to medium low and cook, stirring occasionally, until tender, about 8 minutes.

3. Add the paprika, ginger, turmeric, and cinnamon, and cook, stirring, 1 minute more.

4. Return the chicken to the sauté pan. Stir in the lemon juice and stock. Add the carrots. Bring to a boil, reduce the heat, and simmer, covered, until the chicken breasts are done, about 20 minutes. Transfer to a platter.

5. Arrange the lemon wedges on the platter and serve immediately.

GINGER AND LIME CHICKEN BREASTS WITH MANGO SALSA

4–6 servings

⅓ cup fresh lime juice
2 teaspoons grated fresh ginger
3 garlic cloves, peeled and flattened
½ teaspoon dried red pepper flakes
3 whole chicken breasts (about 1 pound each), boned, skinned, and cut into ½-inch-wide lengthwise strips

Mango Salsa

1 ripe mango, peeled, seeded, and diced
1 small red onion, chopped
¼ cup chopped fresh cilantro
5 tablespoons lime juice
1 tablespoon chopped fresh mint
1 tablespoon olive oil
1 small red serrano chile pepper, seeded and minced
⅛ teaspoon freshly ground black pepper

2 teaspoons olive oil
8 very thin lime slices for garnish
Fresh cilantro sprigs for garnish

1. Mix the lime juice, ginger, garlic, and pepper flakes in a bowl. Add the chicken strips and toss to coat well. Cover and marinate for 2 hours.

2. Combine the mango, onion, cilantro, lime juice, mint, oil, chile pepper, and black pepper in a mixing bowl. Cover with plastic wrap and refrigerate for 2 hours or more. Serve at room temperature.

3. In a sauté pan, heat the oil. Sauté the chicken over medium-high heat until browned, about 4 minutes on each side. Transfer to a platter to keep warm.

4. Add the lime slices to the sauté pan and brown on both sides. Set several on each plate, with a spoonful of fruit salsa next to the chicken. Garnish with sprigs of cilantro.

Q: Is cooking with alcohol the same as drinking it?

A: No. Not at all. The alcohol in any recipe is cooked off, leaving only the flavor essence. When deglazing a pan with wine, if the bottom of the pan is dry, the alcohol will quickly and completely evaporate. Sauces must boil down for the same effect to occur. This is especially important to know for people who, for any of a multitude of reasons, do not consume alcohol. If you're looking for a substitute, try chicken stock, a few tablespoons of lemon juice, or additional herbs reduced in ½ cup of water boiled down to 2 or 3 tablespoons.

CHICKEN BREASTS IN WATERCRESS SAUCE

6 servings

3 whole chicken breasts (about 1 pound each), skinned, boned, and halved
Salt and freshly ground black pepper
2 eggs, beaten well
All-purpose flour for dredging
¼ cup vegetable oil
1 cup dry white wine
1½ cups heavy cream
4 tablespoons (½ stick) cold unsalted butter, cut into small pieces
1 small garlic clove, minced
3 shallots, peeled and minced, or 1 small onion, finely chopped
½ small bunch parsley, stemmed and blanched for 10 seconds
2 small bunches watercress, stemmed and blanched for 5 seconds
1 teaspoon all-purpose flour
Freshly ground black pepper to taste

1. Sprinkle the chicken breasts with salt and pepper. Place the eggs and flour in separate shallow bowls. Dip each piece of chicken in the eggs, then the flour, shaking off any excess.

2. In a sauté pan, heat the oil. Sauté the chicken over medium-high heat until golden brown, about 5 minutes on each side. Transfer to a warmed platter and cover to keep warm.

3. In a saucepan, bring the wine and cream to a boil and reduce by half.

4. In a small sauté pan, melt 1 tablespoon of the butter. Sauté the garlic and shallots until soft but not browned.

5. In a blender or a food processor fitted with a steel blade, combine the cream reduction, parsley, watercress, garlic and shallot mixture. Process until fairly smooth. Add to the sauté pan and cook the sauce over medium-low heat for 2 to 3 minutes. Whisk in the remaining butter a piece at a time. Add salt and freshly ground black pepper to taste.

6. Place the chicken breasts on individual plates, spoon on the sauce, and serve immediately.

Stir Frying

Oh, go for a wok!

Is it because wok cooking is so convenient that it has quietly crept into our kitchens? Its best qualities are what everyone seems to be clamoring for these days—cutting down on the use of oil, and the ability to toss effortlessly together an absolutely delightful dinner in one pan without its tasting like leftover surprise or looking like some unidentifiable hash.

Think of wok cooking, or stir frying, as a technique, rather than the mainstay of Oriental cooking. That way, you can be more inventive with your vegetables, meats, and flavorings. Who's to say you can't use Italian ingredients to make a quick Roman-style stir fry? Go ahead and create something wonderful. Then let me know how it comes out.

CHICKEN BREAST AND SWEET PEPPER STIR FRY

4 servings

1 tablespoon soy sauce
1 tablespoon oyster sauce
2 tablespoons dry sherry
Freshly ground black pepper to taste
3 tablespoons peanut oil
1 medium onion, thinly sliced
2 garlic cloves, chopped
1 whole chicken breast (about 1 pound),
    boned, skinned, and cut into 1-inch
    strips
1 red bell pepper, cored, seeded, and cut
    into thin strips
1 green bell pepper, cored, seeded, and
    cut into thin strips
⅓ cup cashews, toasted golden brown

1. In a small bowl, combine the soy sauce, oyster sauce, sherry, and black pepper.

2. In a wok, heat the oil over high heat until very hot but not smoking. Add the onion and garlic and stir fry for about 3 minutes. Add the chicken and stir fry for 3 minutes more. Add the peppers and cashews. Add the soy sauce mixture and stir fry 2 minutes, or until the peppers are tender.

3. Serve immediately.

Note Oyster sauce is available at Oriental markets or in the Chinese section of the grocery store.

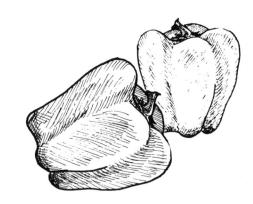

STIR FRY—A DEFINITION

Stir fry is the cooking method most often used in Chinese kitchens all over the world. It is perhaps the most sophisticated cooking method used in the oldest cuisine known to man—Chinese. Essentially, it is cooking in a very small amount of oil over very high heat, stirring constantly so that food is never in contact with the cooking surface longer than a few seconds, or long enough to burn. Simple! With stir frying, vegetables retain their natural color and texture, chicken breasts come out tender and juicy, and the flavoring possibilities are limitless.

STIR-FRIED GINGER CHICKEN

6 servings

1 bunch broccoli, separated into florets
    and the stems sliced
2 cups snow pea pods
1 tablespoon peanut oil
3 whole chicken breasts (about 1 pound
    each), boned, skinned, and cut into
    1-inch strips
2 cups chicken stock (see page 9)
1 2-inch piece of fresh ginger, peeled
    and finely grated
2 garlic cloves, quartered
1 tablespoon cornstarch, mixed with ⅓
    cup cold water
⅓ cup soy sauce
⅓ cup dry sherry
1 teaspoon dark Oriental sesame oil

1. Blanch the broccoli in boiling water for 3 minutes. Run under cold water to stop the cooking process. Repeat with the snow peas for 1 minute. Set aside.

2. In a wok, heat the peanut oil over high heat until very hot but not smoking. Add the chicken and stir fry just until done. Do not overcook. Remove the chicken and set aside.

3. In the wok, combine the stock, ginger, and garlic. Bring to a boil, cook for 5 minutes, then let cool slightly and strain the stock. Return the stock to the wok, stir in the cornstarch mixture, and cook until the mixture thickens. Add the soy sauce, sherry, and sesame oil. Add the chicken and vegetables and heat through. Serve immediately.

Note Oriental sesame oil is available in Oriental markets or in the Chinese section of the grocery store.

THE WELL-SEASONED WOK

Low-carbon-steel woks must be seasoned before they can be used. This is a good project for an afternoon. First, add ½ cup oil to the wok and spread it around to coat the surface evenly. Cook over medium-low heat for 15 minutes, re-coating the surface thoroughly. Discard the oil, wipe the wok clean, and wash it with soap and water. Dry the wok over medium heat. This will keep the wok from rusting. Air-drying the wok after at least the first twenty uses will continue the sealing process. After that, the wok may be wiped dry without fear of rust.

CHICKEN BREAST AND ASIAN OYSTER MUSHROOM SAUCE

4 servings

Sauce

½ cup dry sherry
3 tablespoons light soy sauce
3 tablespoons freshly squeezed lime juice
2 teaspoons sugar

1 tablespoon dark Oriental sesame oil
1 tablespoon vegetable oil
1 tablespoon chopped fresh ginger
¼ teaspoon ground Szechwan pepper
2 cloves garlic, chopped
1 whole chicken breast (about 1 pound), boned, skinned, and cut into 1-inch pieces
4 scallions, cut into 1-inch lengths
2 celery stalks, sliced
¼ pound snow pea pods
1 red bell pepper, stemmed, seeded, and cut julienne
12 dried oyster mushrooms (or other dried mushrooms, like shiitake), submerged in 1 cup boiling water for 15 minutes, stemmed and coarsely chopped
¼ pound fresh mushrooms (white or shiitake), washed, stemmed, and cut into thin slices
1½ teaspoons cornstarch, dissolved in 2 tablespoons cold water

1. In a small bowl, combine the sherry, soy sauce, lime juice, and sugar. Set aside.

2. In a wok, heat the oils over high heat until very hot but not smoking. Add the ginger, garlic, and pepper and stir fry for 30 seconds. Add the chicken and stir fry just until seared on all sides. Remove from the wok and set aside.

3. Add the scallions, celery, snow peas, red pepper, and mushrooms. Stir fry for 2 minutes. Return the chicken pieces to the pan and add the sauce. With the heat on high, cover partially and cook for 2 minutes. Add the cornstarch mixture and stir until slightly thickened, about 1 minute more. Serve immediately.

Note Dried oyster mushrooms are available in Oriental markets or in the Chinese section of the grocery store.

CHILE CHICKEN BREAST STIR FRY

This is a Thai-style dish, so certain ingredients, like bai gaprow, which are fresh holy basil leaves, are available at Thai and some Asian markets. Another unusual ingredient is the famous Thai fish sauce naam pla. Check to make sure you have these ingredients before starting this recipe. It just wouldn't be the same without them. Serve with cooked rice (see page 82).

4 servings

⅓ cup vegetable oil
3 garlic cloves, minced
2 whole chicken breasts (about 1 pound each), boned, skinned, and cut into bite-size pieces
2 red serrano chile peppers, stemmed, seeded, and sliced very thinly cross-wise
¾ cup coarsely chopped scallions
½ cup naam pla
1 tablespoon sugar
¼ cup chopped fresh bai gaprow

1. In a wok, heat the oil over medium-high heat until very hot but not smoking. Add the garlic and stir fry until golden.

Add the chicken and stir fry for 2 to 3 minutes more.

2. Add the chiles, scallions, naam pla, and sugar. Stir fry for about 5 minutes, or until the chicken is done.

3. Add the bai gaprow, toss to mix well, and serve immediately.

Q: Why should you always wear rubber gloves when handling hot chiles?

A: The chiles naturally contain oils. This is where the heat comes from. They are quickly absorbed by the skin, and once they penetrate, no amount of water will cool the burn. It can take many hours for the burning sensation to subside. What's more, any other part of the body, especially the eyes, can be seriously affected by the oil of a chile, so be very careful when handling these flavorful but treacherous little things.

CHICKEN WITH CHINESE LONG BEANS AND WALNUTS STIR FRY

4 servings

1 whole chicken breast (about 1 pound), boned, skinned, and cut into 1-inch strips
¾ teaspoon salt
¾ teaspoon sugar
1 teaspoon light soy sauce
1 teaspoon cornstarch
Dash of black pepper
1 pound Chinese long beans (or string beans), stringed and tips removed, quartered
¼ cup vegetable oil
1 tablespoon Chinese hot bean sauce (available in a jar)
2 teaspoons finely chopped garlic
½ cup chicken stock (see page 9)
2 teaspoons cornstarch, mixed with 2 tablespoons cold water
½ cup walnuts, quartered and toasted until crisp

1. Put the chicken in a bowl. Sprinkle with ½ teaspoon salt, ½ teaspoon sugar, and the soy sauce, cornstarch, and pepper. Mix well and set aside.

2. Boil the beans in lightly salted water along with 1 tablespoon of the oil. Cook for 7 minutes, or until barely tender.

3. Mash the hot bean sauce and garlic to a paste.

4. In a wok, heat 2 tablespoons of the oil over high heat until very hot but not smoking. Add the chicken and stir fry for 2 minutes. Add half of the stock, cover, and cook for 2 minutes. Remove from the wok and set aside.

5. Add the remaining oil to the wok. Add the bean sauce paste and the beans. Stir fry for 2 minutes. Add the remaining salt, sugar, and stock, bring to a boil, and quickly return the chicken to the wok. Add the cornstarch mixture and stir until slightly thickened, about 1 minute more. Remove from the heat, toss in the walnuts, and serve immediately.

Note Chinese long beans are available in Oriental markets or the Chinese section of the grocery store.

PINEAPPLE SESAME CHICKEN BREAST STIR FRY

4 servings

1 egg white, lightly beaten
2½ tablespoons cornstarch
¼ teaspoon baking soda
½ teaspoon baking powder
2 whole chicken breasts (about 1 pound
    each), boned, skinned, and cut into
    1½-inch strips
½ teaspoon salt
½ teaspoon sugar
1 teaspoon light soy sauce
1 teaspoon oyster sauce
Dash of black pepper

Sauce
1 8-ounce can pineapple chunks in juice
1 celery stalk, stringed and cut julienne
½ cup chicken stock
1 tablespoon rice wine vinegar
½ teaspoon sugar

2 cups vegetable oil for deep frying
1 tablespoon cornstarch, mixed with 1
    tablespoon chicken stock
2 tablespoons white sesame seeds, toasted
    in a nonstick pan over medium heat
    until golden brown

1. Put the egg white in a bowl. Mix in the cornstarch, baking soda, baking powder, and 1 tablespoon cold water. Let stand at least 5 hours, or overnight.

2. Put the chicken in a bowl. Sprinkle on the salt, sugar, soy sauce, oyster sauce, and pepper. Mix well to combine.

3. To make the sauce, in a saucepan, combine the pineapple and its juice with the celery, stock, vinegar, and sugar. Slowly bring to a boil. Remove from the heat and set aside.

4. In a wok, heat the oil over high heat until very hot but not smoking. Add the chicken pieces to the batter and coat completely. Drop the pieces into the oil a few at a time, tossing with a slotted spatula to make sure the chicken doesn't stick. Deep fry each batch for about 3 minutes. Drain on paper towels if desired. Arrange in a serving bowl.

5. Reheat the pineapple sauce. Add the cornstarch mixture and cook until it thickens, about 1 minute. Pour over the hot chicken and serve immediately, sprinkled with sesame seeds.

Note Oyster sauce is available in Oriental markets or in the Chinese section of the grocery store.

CASHEW CHICKEN BREAST STIR FRY

4 servings

1 whole chicken breast (about 1 pound),
    skinned, boned, and cut into ½-inch
    pieces
¾ teaspoon salt
¾ teaspoon sugar
1 teaspoon soy sauce
1 teaspoon oyster sauce
1 tablespoon cornstarch
2 tablespoons vegetable oil
1 celery stalk, strings removed, cut into
    1½-inch pieces lengthwise and then
    cut julienne
½ yellow onion, cut into 8 wedges
1 carrot, peeled and thinly sliced
½ cup thinly sliced mushrooms
1 cup chicken stock (see page 9)
¾ cup canned sliced bamboo shoots
1 tablespoon cornstarch, mixed with 1
    tablespoon chicken stock
2 teaspoons dark Oriental sesame oil
½ cup unsalted roasted cashews

1. Put the chicken in a bowl. Sprinkle on ½ teaspoon of the salt, ½ teaspoon of the sugar, and the soy sauce, oyster sauce, and cornstarch. Mix well and set aside.

2. In a wok, heat 1 tablespoon of the oil over high heat until very hot but not smoking. Add the celery, onion, carrot, and mushrooms and stir fry for 2 minutes. Add the remaining salt and sugar, and toss to mix well. Quickly remove the vegetables from the wok and set aside.

3. In the wok, heat the remaining tablespoon of the oil in the wok over high heat until very hot but not smoking. Add the chicken and stir fry for 2 minutes. Add the stock, reserving 1 tablespoon, and bamboo shoots, toss to mix, cover, and cook for 3 minutes.

4. Add the cornstarch mixture. Stir until slightly thickened, about 1 minute more. Remove from the heat. Toss in the sesame oil and cashews. Serve immediately.

Note Oyster sauce is available in Oriental markets or in the Chinese section of the grocery store.

A WOK IS A WOK IS A WOK?

It's not! If you intend to develop a repertoire of stir-fry dishes, the best wok you can buy is a hand-pounded low-carbon-steel wok made in China. These woks are available in Oriental markets. Though they are much more expensive than the American machine-made steel woks, any skilled Chinese chef will tell you it is their thickness—usually twice as thick as the machine-made—that keeps the food from burning on the amazingly hard carbon surface. Stainless-steel woks are available but require too much oil to keep the food from sticking. Electric woks turn everything into mush and seldom stay hot enough for successful stir frying. Wok cooking on electric stoves is possible if the smallest burner is used at the highest heat. But for the best results, use a hand-pounded low-carbon-steel wok over a gas flame.

Since cooking in a wok is done only in the bottom of the pan, a "chan," or spatula that is rounded across the bottom, and a long-handled ladle are essential tools for tossing and pushing the stir-frying food against the sides of the pan to prevent overcooking. A lid is also useful, for steaming vegetables that are arranged around the sides of the wok, with only a little water boiling in the center.

OIL: THE NUMBER ONE INGREDIENT

I always wondered what type of oil was best to use when stir frying. Vegetable oil is called for in many recipes, but vegetable oil could mean anything. So here is the final word on oils in the wok. Use only oils that can withstand the high temperatures required for stir-fry cooking—peanut, safflower, and corn oil, in that order, are the first choices of experienced stir-fry cooks. Butter and olive oil begin to burn before reaching the high temperatures needed. Oils used as flavorings, such as dark Oriental sesame oil, are added after the entire cooking process is completed and the dish is ready to be turned out onto a serving platter.

Q: **What type of pan makes a good substitute for a wok?**

A: **In a pinch, a large heavy cast-iron skillet or stainless-steel frying pan can be used. But there's nothing like a wok for its ability to cook foods quickly over high heat with very little oil.**

PERFECT RICE: BROWN, WHITE, OR WILD

I found myself bored with just plain old steamed rice, so I started boiling my white or brown rice with seasonings—another chance to be creative. For each cup of white rice, bring approximately 3 cups water (or more) and ¼ teaspoon salt to a full boil. Add dried herbs, parsley, or some salt-free vegetable seasoning (i.e., Spike or Mrs. Dash). Test the rice after 10 to 12 minutes. Do not overcook. Drain the rice in a colander. Since much of the starch stays in the water, immediately rinse the cooked rice with hot tap water, then drain for 2 or 3 minutes. Rice cooked this way is always fluffy and is a perfect Chinese stir-fry accompaniment, as well as a sensational addition to salads. Substituting wild rice (not rice but a grass) is another approach to satisfying the rice portion of a meal. Wild rice, with its unusual nutlike flavor, is also a great tasty diet food, since it is low in starch, fat, and calories. Wild rice requires soaking and long cooking, so package directions should be followed.

If perfect steamed white rice is your desire, here are the simple instructions: Put 1 cup long-grain white rice in a heavy saucepan. Cover with water and drain to rinse the rice. Add 1¾ cups cold water and ½ teaspoon salt to the pan. Bring to a boil, cook for 2 minutes, then cover the saucepan, reduce the heat to very low, and cook for 20 minutes. Remove the rice from the heat and let it stand, covered, for 10 minutes. Stir to separate and fluff the grains before serving. Brown rice can be cooked in the same way, using 1 cup rice and 2 cups water, though it takes longer to cook through.

Baking

In between the making, when you're baking, there's always a little time to sit down with a glass of wine

Chicken breasts are quick to fix, no matter what the cooking technique. Baking is no exception. When you think of the lengthy cooking time for a turkey, or even a meat loaf, this perfect white meat proves to be a treasure in itself over and over again. Many recipes in this section can be prepared ahead of time, then assembled for cooking as needed. Unlike sauté or stir-fry recipes, these tend to take a little longer on the preparation end, but once the dish is in the oven, you're off the hook and out of the kitchen. These one-dish concepts are truly time-savers, especially for entertaining.

BAKED CHICKEN WITH TOMATO MUSTARD CREAM SAUCE

This recipe offers an opportunity to show off your culinary skills. The sauce, tangy yet creamy, is a perfect complement to the delicate meat of the chicken breast. Using crème fraîche in the sauce makes it a bit lighter than with heavy cream, though the calories are the same.

4 servings

2 whole chicken breasts (about 1 pound each), boned, skinned, and halved
Salt and freshly ground black pepper

Sauce
3 tablespoons olive oil
5 large ripe tomatoes, peeled, seeded, and finely diced
1 tablespoon minced fresh thyme, or 1 teaspoon dried thyme
Salt and freshly ground black pepper to taste
3 tablespoons dry white wine
3 tablespoons white wine vinegar
1½ tablespoons finely chopped shallots
1 tablespoon grainy mustard
1½ cups crème fraîche or heavy cream
6 tablespoons (¾ stick) cold unsalted butter, cut into small pieces

1. Cut the chicken breasts at a 30-degree angle across the grain into ½-inch-thick slices. Sprinkle with salt and pepper. Place on an oiled heavy baking sheet. Refrigerate until ready to cook.

2. In a sauté pan, heat the oil. Add the tomatoes and cook over moderately high heat, stirring constantly, for about 7 minutes, or until thick and well reduced. Add the thyme and salt and pepper. Remove from the heat and set aside.

3. Preheat the oven to 450° F.

4. In a heavy nonreactive saucepan, bring the wine, vinegar, and shallots to a boil over medium-high heat. Continue boiling until almost all the liquid is evaporated. Remove the pan from the heat, whisk in the mustard and crème fraîche, and return to the heat, cooking until reduced by half. Add the butter, a piece at a time, whisking constantly. When the mixture is thick and foamy, combine with the tomato reduction. Taste for salt and pepper. Keep warm.

5. Bake the chicken breasts for 14 minutes. Do not overcook. Reheat the sauce.

6. Arrange the chicken breasts on individual plates and spoon on the sauce. Serve immediately with the remaining sauce on the side.

QUICK CHICKEN AND VEGGIE CASSEROLE

Thanks to Herb Zwieg for this recipe. He recommends serving it with parsley-laced couscous (the Near Eastern equivalent of pasta) on the side.

4 servings

2 whole chicken breasts (about 1 pound each), skinned, boned, and cut into 1-inch chunks
⅓ cup all-purpose flour
½ teaspoon dried sage
¾ teaspoon freshly ground black pepper
1 teaspoon onion powder
2 tablespoons extra-virgin olive oil
2 green bell peppers, seeded and cut into large chunks
2 red bell peppers, seeded and cut into large chunks
1 large zucchini, cut into ½-inch-thick slices
½ cup chicken stock (see page 9)
1 cup white wine
Juice of 2 limes
1 2-inch piece of fresh ginger, peeled and grated
6 slices mozzarella cheese

1. Put the chicken in a bowl.

2. In a small bowl, mix together the flour, sage, black pepper, and onion powder. Rub the seasonings into the chicken chunks with your hands.

3. In an ovenproof baking pan or Dutch oven, heat the oil. Add the chicken pieces and brown quickly over medium-high heat. Remove the chicken to a plate.

4. Add the peppers and zucchini to the pan. Cook, stirring frequently, for 2 to 3 minutes. Remove the pan from the heat and add the chicken, stock, wine, lime juice, and ginger.

5. Place the mozzarella slices on top. Cover and bake for 30 minutes. Serve immediately.

ONION, LEEK, CHICKEN, AND CHEESE TORTE

This take-along torte is positively a picnic favorite. For potluck affairs, this can be easily re-heated in a microwave, or served at room temperature. Or just add a salad and serve piping hot from the oven for a lovely Sunday brunch selection instead of the standard quiche.

1 9-inch torte

Pastry
2 cups sifted all-purpose flour
½ teaspoon salt
½ cup (1 stick) cold unsalted butter, cut into small pieces
1 egg
1 egg yolk
¼ cup milk
2 tablespoons chopped fresh parsley

2 tablespoons unsalted butter
2 cups chopped leeks (white part only)
1 large onion, coarsely chopped
4 shallots, chopped
1 whole chicken breast (about 1 pound), boned, skinned, and thinly sliced against the grain
3 eggs
1½ cups ricotta cheese
1 cup chopped fresh parsley

8 pieces green leek tops, blanched for 15 seconds in boiling water

1. In a food processor fitted with a steel blade, combine the flour, salt, and butter. Pulse the mixture until very coarse (it will look like cornmeal).

2. Add the egg and yolk and mix well. Add the milk and parsley and continue pulsing until the pastry forms a ball on the sides of the bowl. Remove and refrigerate for at least 2 hours.

3. To make the filling, in a heavy saucepan, melt the butter. Add the chopped leeks and onion. Sauté over medium-low heat until soft. Add the shallots and continue sautéing for 2 or 3 minutes more. Remove from the pan and set aside. Add the chicken to the pan and sauté over medium heat for 2 to 3 minutes. Do not cook completely. Set aside.

4. Preheat the oven to 375° F.

5. Remove the pastry dough from the refrigerator and roll into a circle large enough to cover the bottom and sides of a 9-inch springform pan. Put the dough in the pan and refrigerate again.

6. In a small bowl, mix together the eggs, ricotta, and parsley. Layer the leek mixture, chicken pieces, and the ricotta mixture in the torte pan. Decorate the top of the torte with the leek tops (e.g., in a lattice pattern or as the spokes of a wheel).

7. Bake for 50 minutes to 1 hour, or until the cheese is set and the crust is golden. Serve warm or at room temperature.

CALIFORNIA-STYLE HERB AND GOAT CHEESE– FILLED CHICKEN BREASTS

Elegant party fare!

4 servings

2 whole chicken breasts (about 1 pound each), boned, and cartilage removed
½ pound domestic or imported goat cheese (chèvre), at room temperature
1 tablespoon finely chopped fresh oregano
1 tablespoon finely chopped fresh thyme
1 large garlic clove, finely minced
¼ teaspoon salt
½ teaspoon freshly ground white pepper
1 tablespoon extra-virgin olive oil
1 cup Chardonnay or other good dry white wine

1. Preheat the oven to 375° F.

2. Loosen the skin from the chicken breasts just enough to form a pocket, leaving the skin partially attached.

3. In a small bowl, combine the cheese, herbs, garlic, salt, and pepper.

4. Divide the filling between the breasts and tuck under the skin. Pull the skin over and around the filling; tuck all the edges of the meat under to form a neat little package. Arrange the breasts in an oiled glass baking dish.

5. Sprinkle the breasts with salt and pepper to taste and brush the tops with oil. Roast for 25 to 35 minutes, or until golden brown.

6. Pour any excess fat from the pan. Place the pan over medium-high heat. Add the wine and deglaze, scraping up any browned bits as the sauce reduces. Cook until slightly thickened. Strain the sauce if necessary; serve on the side.

MEXICAN CHILEQUIDES

This is another recipe that travels well and is delicious served hot or at room temperature. Up to step 5, you can prepare this Mexical casserole type dish one day in advance. Just cover with plastic wrap and refrigerate. One hour before you're ready to cook the chilequides, remove the dish from the refrigerator. Consider using this even as a starter (see page 13).

4–6 servings

2 tablespoons (¼ stick) unsalted butter
1 onion, coarsely chopped
5 medium tomatoes, peeled, seeded, and coarsely chopped
1 cup fresh cilantro
2 garlic cloves
2 serrano chiles, stemmed and seeded
Salt to taste
Vegetable oil for frying
8 6-inch corn tortillas
2 whole chicken breasts (about 1 pound each), skinned, boned, and grilled (see page 103 for instructions) and sliced into ¼ inch julienne
1 cup sour cream, at room temperature
1½ cups freshly grated queso anejo (dry, aged white Mexican cheese)
⅔ cup chicken stock (see page 9)

1. In a large heavy saucepan over medium heat, melt the butter. Add the onion and sauté until translucent, about 5 minutes. Transfer the onion to a food processor fitted with a steel blade. Add the tomatoes, cilantro, garlic, and chiles. Process to the consistency of salsa.

2. Return the mixture to the saucepan. Bring to a boil. Reduce the heat and, stirring occasionally, simmer until slightly thickened, about 20 minutes. Taste for salt.

3. Preheat the oven to 350° F.

4. Heat ½ inch oil in a large heavy skillet. Cook the tortillas one at a time until golden brown, about 2 minutes per side. Drain on paper towel.

5. In the bottom of a 9 x 13-inch baking dish, overlap 3 of the tortillas. Top with a third of the salsa, a third of the sour cream, a third of the chicken, and a third of the cheese. Repeat the layers.

6. Pour the stock over the layers and bake about 35 minutes, or until the top is brown and bubbling. Serve immediately or warm.

CHICKEN BREAST AND SPINACH LOAF

A great buffet dish as well as a magnificent main course. This loaf looks wonderful when placed in the center of a white plate and garnished with sprigs of herbs all around. It also can be served as a starter (see page 13).

6–8 servings

2 whole chicken breasts (about 1 pound each), skinned, boned, and chopped
2 pounds fresh spinach, washed well, stemmed, and chopped, or 1 10-ounce package frozen chopped spinach, thawed and drained well
¾ cup finely chopped carrots
1 cup finely chopped onion
5 eggs, lightly beaten
½ cup tomato paste
1 teaspoon salt
¾ teaspoon freshly ground black pepper
1 cup seasoned fine dry bread crumbs

1. Preheat the oven to 375° F.

2. In a large mixing bowl, combine the chicken, spinach, carrots, and onion.

3. In another bowl, beat together the eggs, tomato paste, salt, and pepper. Stir into the chicken mixture to combine well. Fold in the bread crumbs. Do not overmix.

4. Line 2 loaf pans with parchment paper and gently spoon in the chicken mixture, being careful not to pack it down, making the mixture too dense.

5. Bake 40 to 50 minutes, or until the internal temperature reaches 140° F. on a meat thermometer.

6. Let cool slightly and serve from the pan, or wait 15 minutes before unmolding.

CHICKEN BREAST ENCHILADAS WITH MILD GREEN CHILI SAUCE

6 servings

Poaching liquid: 2 cups (or more) chicken stock (see page 9), 1 cilantro sprig, 1 parsley sprig, pinch of salt, 1 bay leaf

2 whole chicken breasts (about 1 pound each)

Green Chili Sauce

20 fresh tomatillos (Mexican green tomatoes), or 2 1- to 3-ounce cans tomatillos

¼ cup vegetable oil

1½ cups chopped onion

6 Anaheim chile peppers, or 1 7-ounce can mild chile peppers, drained and chopped

2 large garlic cloves, pressed

2 tablespoons minced fresh oregano, or 2 teaspoons finely crumbled dried oregano

2 tablespoons freshly squeezed lemon juice

1 teaspoon sugar

1 teaspoon salt

2 cups chicken stock (see page 9) or strained poaching liquid

2 bay leaves

2 cups shredded Monterey Jack cheese

1 tablespoon minced fresh or 1 teaspoon dried oregano

12 corn tortillas

Vegetable oil for frying

Avocado slices or guacamole for garnish

Chopped ripe tomatoes for garnish

Sour cream for garnish

Ripe olives for garnish

Cilantro leaves for garnish

Spicy green chile salsa or tomato salsa (see page 14)

1. In a large saucepan or stockpot, bring the poaching liquid to a boil. Add the chicken breasts, arrange in a single layer, and cover. Simmer for 8 to 10 minutes, or just until the pink color is gone throughout. The breasts will be firm when pressed with the back of a fork. Let cool to room temperature in the stock. Remove the skin and bones, and shred the chicken into bite-size pieces.

2. Put the tomatillos in a saucepan and cover with water. Over medium-high heat, bring to a boil and cook until almost tender, about 5 minutes. Drain in a colander, rinse, and drain again. Set aside. (If using canned tomatillos, just drain and set aside.)

3. In a heavy skillet, heat the oil. Add the onion and cook over medium-high heat until translucent, about 5 minutes. Transfer to a blender or a food processor fitted with a steel blade. Add the tomatillos, chiles, garlic, 2 tablespoons oregano, lemon juice, sugar, salt, and half of the stock. Process until smooth.

4. Transfer the mixture to a saucepan, add the remaining stock and the bay leaves, and bring to a boil. Reduce the heat to low, cover, and simmer until the sauce is slightly thickened, about 30 minutes. Remove the bay leaves. Set aside.

5. Preheat the oven to 350° F.

6. In a bowl, combine the chicken, 1½ cups cheese, and 1 tablespoon fresh oregano. Set aside.

7. Reheat the chili sauce. Pour vegetable oil into a 10-inch skillet to a depth of ½ inch. One at a time over medium heat, fry the tortillas for just a few seconds, then dip immediately and briefly in the chili sauce and let the excess drain off. Lay each tortilla on a flat surface, spoon ⅓ to ½ cup of the chicken filling down the center, roll up into a cylinder, and place, seam side down, in an oven-proof dish. Spoon a little of the sauce over the tops of the enchiladas. Cover with foil.

A little less chicken

8. Bake about 15 minutes, or until the filling is heated through. Remove the foil, sprinkle on the remaining cheese over the enchiladas, and bake about 10 minutes, or until the cheese is melted.

9. Heat 6 plates. Spoon some chili sauce onto each and put 2 hot enchiladas on the sauce. Garnish with avocado slices, chopped tomatoes, sour cream, olives, and cilantro. Pass the spicy salsa on the side.

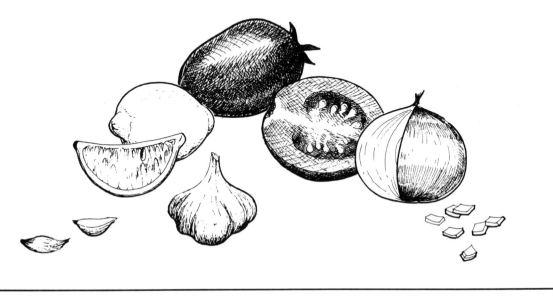

BREAST OF FREE-RANGE CHICKEN FLORENTINE

The Beverly Hills Hotel, towering pink and pristine above the palms on Sunset Boulevard, has become a legend in its own time. It was built when the Old West was slowly fading into the sunset and the great stars of Hollywood peered over the horizon. The original beauty of 1912 still remains. There is, however, one place at the Beverly Hills Hotel where change rushed in only two years ago—the kitchen!

Michel Saragueta took over as executive chef, fresh from New York and the also famed "21." This is one of Michel's favorite simple but incredibly delicious dishes, very popular at power lunches in the Polo Lounge, where folks from the film business (among others) congregate.

4 servings

2 whole breasts of free-range chicken
    (about 1 pound each), skinned,
    boned, and halved
¼ cup olive oil

2 bunches spinach, washed, dried,
    stemmed, and chopped
Salt and freshly ground black pepper to
    taste
½ cup freshly grated Monterey Jack
    cheese
1 cup heavy cream
2 tablespoons minced fresh basil
2 tablespoons minced fresh chives

1. With a sharp, pointed knife make an incision in the thickest end of the breast. Do not cut all the way through.

2. In a sauté pan, heat 1 tablespoon of the oil. Add the spinach and salt and pepper, and sauté over medium-high heat just until the spinach is wilted, about 2 minutes. Remove to a plate to cool. Squeeze the moisture out of the spinach. Mix in the cheese.

3. Arrange the breasts on a work surface. Fill the pockets carefully with the spinach mixture. Roll each breast in plastic wrap to make a sausage shape. Remove the plastic wrap.

4. Preheat the oven to 375° F.

5. In a sauté pan, heat the remaining oil. Sauté the chicken breasts until golden brown on all sides, about 5 minutes. Transfer to a baking dish and bake 10 minutes, or until done.

6. Pour off any excess oil from the pan. Deglaze the pan with the cream, cooking over medium-high heat until slightly reduced. Lower the heat and add the herbs. Stir and cook for 1 minute more.

Taste for salt and pepper.

7. Slice the chicken breasts in rounds on the diagonal. Pour sauce on 4 warmed plates. Set the chicken breasts on the sauce and serve immediately.

PARMESAN-CRUSTED CHICKEN BREASTS

Very Good

Positively perfect picnic or backyard lunch fare.

2 to 3 serv or 1 serv

4–6 servings

½ cup Dijon mustard *¼ c ⅛*
¼ cup dry white wine *⅛ c 1/16*
1 cup fresh bread crumbs
1 cup finely grated Parmesan cheese *½*
    (best quality) *or ¼*
3 whole chicken breasts (about 1 pound
    each), boned, skinned, and split

*used
(2) 5 m
½ breasts
from
— most of isn't fell*

*But I made
without cheese*

1. Preheat the oven to 375° F.

2. In a shallow bowl, whisk the mustard and wine. The mixture should be a dipping consistency. Set aside.

3. Combine the bread crumbs and cheese. Dip the chicken breasts in the mustard mixture, then roll in the crumbs.

4. Bake on a greased baking sheet for 30 minutes, or until the chicken is cooked through and the coating is brown and crispy. Serve hot or at room temperature.

*Had to cook
20 min longer, but
oven cooks odd
sometime*

93

LOBSTER-FILLED CHICKEN BREAST WITH BLACK BEAN SAUCE

This is a very special recipe, the kind of dish you'd order in one of the finest restaurants imaginable. Bill Higgins, executive chef at Dux in the elegant Peabody Hotel in Orlando, Florida, passed this recipe along to me, but only after I had ordered it several times to prove my devotion to his inventive and extraordinary combination of flavors.

4 servings

1 2-pound lobster, tail meat removed and cut into quarters lengthwise
2 whole chicken breasts (about 1 pound each), boned, skinned, halved, and lightly pounded between plastic wrap
Salt and freshly ground black pepper

Black Bean Sauce

1 cup black beans, soaked overnight and drained
½ onion, halved
½ carrot, peeled and quartered
1 1-inch piece of fresh ginger, peeled and minced
2 large garlic cloves, chopped

Lobster Stock

Oil for cooking lobster shells
Shell of one whole lobster including head, pounded
1 onion, coarsely chopped
1 small carrot, coarsely chopped
2 tomatoes, chopped
2 tablespoons olive oil
¼ cup brandy

1 tablespoon olive oil
1 teaspoon rice wine vinegar
½ tablespoon dark Oriental sesame oil
1 teaspoon unsalted butter

1 egg, lightly beaten with 2 tablespoons milk
All-purpose flour
1 cup fine dry seasoned bread crumbs
Chopped cilantro and chives for garnish

1. Sprinkle salt and pepper on the chicken breasts.

2. Place a lobster tail quarter on the end of each chicken breast half, tuck in the edges, and roll around the lobster. Close up the ends with toothpicks and refrigerate.

3. In a saucepan over medium-high heat, cook the beans in water with the onion and carrot until tender. Remove

...beans. Use a ...to make a ...rge ...ount of ...ll. Sauté ...oes. back of ...e vege- randy. ...er the ...im- ...k ...hed ...the

...aste ...or un- Add about ...lobster stock. Add the vinegar, sesame oil, and butter. Set aside.

7. Preheat the oven to 400° F.

8. Put the egg wash in a shallow dish, flour in another, and the bread crumbs in a third. Lightly dust the chicken breasts with flour, gently dip in the egg wash, and roll in bread crumbs.

9. In a sauté pan, heat the olive oil. Lightly brown the chicken on all sides over medium-low heat for 2 to 3 minutes only. Transfer to a baking dish and bake for 8 to 10 minutes, or just until done. Remove from the oven and let rest before cutting into diagonal slices, or serve whole chicken breast rolls.

10. To assemble the plate, spoon some of the hot black bean sauce onto the bottom. Arrange the chicken breast slices over the sauce. Sprinkle on the cilantro and chives. Serve immediately.

VARIATION Shrimp-Filled Chicken Breasts with Black Bean Sauce. Substitute 4 large shrimps, peeled and deveined, for the lobster tail quarters.

CHICKEN MOUSSE WITH TOMATO BASIL SAUCE

This recipe can easily be doubled, and baked in a loaf pan rather than in individual cups. Allow a terrine to rest for at least 30 minutes before slicing.

4 servings

1¼ pounds chicken breast meat, cut into pieces
5 large eggs
4 large egg yolks
1 cup heavy cream
½ teaspoon salt
½ teaspoon freshly ground white pepper
Pinch of nutmeg
1 ounce prosciutto, finely chopped
Melted unsalted butter
8 very thin slices boiled ham (about ¼ pound)

Tomato Basil Sauce
1 tablespoon olive oil
4 ripe tomatoes (about 2 pounds), peeled, seeded, and diced
Bouquet garni: 1 thyme sprig, 1 bay leaf, 1 parsley sprig
½ cup chicken stock, reduced by half (see page 9)
Salt and freshly ground white pepper to taste
3 tablespoons chopped fresh basil or parsley (or a combination of both)

1 tablespoon unsalted butter

1 tablespoon chopped fresh parsley for garnish
1 tablespoon snipped fresh chives for garnish

1. Preheat the oven to 325° F.

2. In two batches, in a blender or a food processor fitted with a steel blade, combine the chicken with the eggs, yolks, cream, salt, pepper, and nutmeg. Process to a smooth paste. Add the prosciutto to the mousse and pulse to mix well.

3. Brush 4 individual custard cups with melted butter. Press 2 slices of ham into each cup so the edges fall a bit over the sides. Pour in the mousse and fold the ham over the top to cover it. Cut 4 rounds of parchment paper to fit the molds. Butter the parchment paper and put it butter side down over the ham.

4. Put the molds in a large baking pan and add water halfway up the sides of the cups. Bake for 40 to 45 minutes, or until the mousse is set.

5. In a saucepan, combine the oil, tomatoes, bouquet garni, and stock. Bring to a simmer and cook for 15 minutes. Remove the bouquet garni and pour the sauce through a strainer into another saucepan. Add salt and pepper, and stir in the basil. Set aside.

6. Remove the molds from the oven and take off the parchment paper. Let cool slightly. Unmold onto individual plates or a serving platter.

7. Add the 1 tablespoon butter to the warm tomato sauce, whisking constantly until it melts. Pour the sauce around the base of the molds. Sprinkle on the parsley and chives. Serve immediately.

PESTO CHICKEN BREASTS

6 servings

2 cups tightly packed fresh basil leaves
⅓ cup finely chopped toasted pine nuts
3 garlic cloves, finely chopped
¾ cup freshly grated Parmesan cheese
½ cup olive oil
3 whole chicken breasts (about 1 pound each), boned and split
Salt and freshly ground black pepper to taste

1. Preheat the oven to 350° F.

2. In a food processor fitted with a steel blade, process the basil until finely chopped. Add the pine nuts, garlic, and cheese. With the motor running, pour in the oil and pulse just until the ingredients are combined.

3. Loosen the skin of each chicken breast enough to form a pocket, leaving the skin partially attached. Divide the pesto between the breasts and tuck under the skin. Pull the skin and meat around the filling to form a little package.

4. Arrange the breasts in an oiled glass baking dish. Sprinkle with salt and pepper and brush with a little olive oil. Bake 25 to 30 minutes, or until golden brown. Serve hot or at room temperature.

SPICY OVEN-FRIED CHICKEN BREASTS

The crispy coating on the chicken is really "hot stuff"! If you prefer a milder flavor, choose another recipe.

4–6 servings

¾ cup fine dry bread crumbs
1½ teaspoons ground cumin
1½ teaspoons crumbled dried oregano
1½ teaspoons salt
¼ teaspoon freshly ground black pepper
½ teaspoon chili powder
⅛ teaspoon cayenne pepper
1 cup all-purpose flour
3 eggs
3½ tablespoons fresh lime juice
3 whole chicken breasts (about 1 pound each), skinned, boned, and split
3 tablespoons unsalted butter
3 tablespoons vegetable oil
Italian flat-leaf parsley for garnish
Lime wedges

1. Preheat the oven to 350° F.

2. In a small bowl, combine the bread crumbs, cumin, oregano, salt, black pepper, chili powder, and cayenne. Put the mixture in a shallow dish.

3. Put the flour in another shallow dish.

4. In a medium bowl, beat the eggs and lime juice together.

5. Roll the chicken breasts in the flour, then dip in the egg mixture, allowing any excess to drip off. Roll in the bread crumb mixture, coating completely. Refrigerate the breasts for at least 30 minutes.

6. In a large heavy skillet, melt half the butter with half the oil over medium heat. Lightly brown half the chicken breasts on both sides. Repeat with the remaining butter and oil. Transfer the breasts to a baking dish.

7. Bake the breasts until cooked throughout and crispy on the outside, 20 to 30 minutes. Garnish with parsley and lime wedges for squeezing.

Grilling

Reawakening the thrill of the grill

It's not just a charcoal-and-lighter-fluid affair anymore. A barbecue is now an all-in-one grill, and smoker if you please. It's also a great place to toast French bread slices and roast cloves of garlic and vegetables (e.g., tomatoes for smoked tomato sauce). It undoubtedly is the best of all cooking methods in any seasons, weather permitting. And lovely are the flavors that can be combined in marinades to make the most magnificent-tasting grilled foods. Grilling is always welcomed for out-of-doors social occasions, providing extraordinary and uniquely flavored fare for family and friends. And for the cleanup crew, what a thrill: no pots, no pans, no hot kitchen to clean.

SPICY FAJITAS FROM THE GRILL

For a spectacular summer sandwich, quick-grill pounded chicken breasts and slice them onto warmed flour tortillas, along with grilled vegetables, guacamole, sour cream, sautéed onions, or chopped cilantro, as desired.

8 servings

¼ cup red wine vinegar
1 tablespoon olive oil
2 garlic cloves, peeled
½ teaspoon ground coriander
½ teaspoon ground cinnamon
½ teaspoon thyme
½ teaspoon salt
¼ teaspoon ground cloves
¼ teaspoon freshly ground black pepper
2 whole chicken breasts (about 1 pound each), skinned, boned, and pounded to ⅓ inch thick
1 large red onion, cut into ¼-inch slices
8 flour tortillas
1 cup fresh tomato salsa (see page 14)

1. Put the vinegar, oil, garlic, herbs, salt, and spices in a blender or food processor and process until well blended. Pour into a glass casserole.

2. Add the chicken breasts and toss to coat well. Marinate for 4 hours, covered, in the refrigerator. Let the chicken breasts stand at room temperature for half an hour before grilling.

3. Prepare a charcoal fire. When the coals are glowing hot with a layer of white ash, grill the chicken breasts 6 to 8 inches from the heat. Cook for 20 minutes, turning every 5 minutes until done.

4. While the chicken is grilling, place the onion slices around the outer rim of the grill and cook until tender. Slice the chicken breasts into strips. Place the tortillas on the grill and warm for 1 minute. Place several slices of chicken, with onion and salsa, on each tortilla and roll up. Serve immediately.

Q: **Which woods add flavor to your barbecue fire?**

A: **Hawaiian kiawe, mesquite, hickory, cherry, apple, maple, oak, walnut, and grapevine cuttings.**

CITRUS AND SPICE GRILLED CHICKEN BREASTS

4–6 servings

2 cups freshly squeezed orange juice, reduced to 1 cup (or 1 cup frozen orange juice concentrate, thawed)
½ cup tomato purée
3 tablespoons honey
2 teaspoons orange zest
1 teaspoon minced lemon zest
½ teaspoon minced lime zest
¼ cup fresh lemon juice
¼ cup fresh lime juice
3 large garlic cloves, pressed
1 teaspoon dried thyme
½ teaspoon cayenne pepper
¾ teaspoon freshly ground black pepper
½ teaspoon salt
3 whole chicken breasts (about 1 pound each), halved

1. In a large bowl, combine the orange juice, tomato purée, honey, zests, lemon and lime juices, garlic, thyme, cayenne, black pepper, and salt. Mix well.

2. Place the chicken breasts in a shallow glass baking dish. Pour on the marinade. Refrigerate, covered with plastic wrap, 12 hours or overnight. Let the chicken stand at room temperature for half an hour before grilling.

3. Prepare a charcoal fire.

4. Drain the chicken, straining the marinade into a small saucepan. Bring the marinade to a boil and cook for 2 minutes.

5. When the coals are glowing with a layer of white ash, grill the chicken breasts 6 to 8 inches from the heat. Cook for 20 minutes, turning and basting every 5 minutes until done. Serve immediately or at room temperature.

A NEW TWIST ON GRILLING AND SMOKING—SPIKED WOOD CHIPS!

The Jack Daniels whiskey distillery in Lynchburg, Tennessee, is now licensing Nature-Glo Brand Charcoal Briquets and Barrel Chunks—briquets formed out of local sugar maple wood and pulverized white oak barrels once used to age their famous alcohol. The briquets, which sell for about $3.25 per seven-pound bag, lend an "outdoorsy" flavor to food, and with nary a trace of whiskey breath.

GRILLED BALSAMIC CHICKEN BREASTS

6–8 servings

4 whole chicken breasts (about 1 pound each), skinned, halved, and flattened to about ¾ inch thick
½ cup balsamic vinegar
4 shallots, chopped
1 teaspoon chopped fresh thyme
2 garlic cloves, pressed
Salt and freshly ground white pepper

Vinaigrette
1 cup chicken stock, reduced to ½ cup (see page 9)
½ cup dry white wine, reduced to ¼ cup (stock and wine may be reduced together)
⅓ cup balsamic vinegar
3 shallots, minced
1 large garlic clove, finely chopped
1 teaspoon chopped fresh thyme, or ½ teaspoon crumbled dried thyme
1 small tomato, peeled, seeded, and very finely chopped
Salt and freshly ground black pepper to taste
1 teaspoon chopped fresh parsley

1. Put the chicken breasts in a shallow glass baking dish. Add the vinegar, shallots, thyme, and garlic. Sprinkle with salt and pepper. Refrigerate, covered with plastic wrap, for at least 2 hours or overnight. Let stand at room temperature for half an hour before grilling.

2. To make the vinaigrette, in a saucepan, combined the stock and wine with the vinegar, shallots, garlic, and thyme. Bring to a boil. Stir in the tomato. Season with salt and pepper. Cook for 2 minutes to reduce and thicken slightly. Set aside.

3. Prepare a charcoal fire. When the coals are glowing with a layer of white ash, place the chicken breasts on the grill, 6 to 8 inches from the heat. Turning every 5 minutes, cook for 20 minutes, or until done.

4. Reheat the vinaigrette. Stir in the parsley and spoon over the chicken breasts. Serve immediately.

SHARPEN YOUR GRILL SKILLS

It doesn't really matter whether you're using a simple hibachi or a fancy outdoor cooker. Here are surefire tips for success:

1. The coals: Use wood chips and hardwood charcoal to fuel your fire. Mesquite, oak, hickory, alder, beech, and fruitwoods (cherry, apple, pecan, and grapevine) infuse foods with robust to delicate smoky flavors. Charcoal briquets may be included along with wood chips, up to half of the total fuel. Of course, the ideal grilling fire would be composed completely of aromatic wood.

2. Building the fire: Successful grilling depends on steady cooking—coals that are not hot enough to give off even heat will char food before cooking it through. Here are two fire-building methods guaranteed not to fizzle out:
   - For a hardwood fire, make a bed of tightly crumbled newspaper (about 10 sheets). Top with a layer of wood kindling and 15 to 25 hardwood chunks (depending on grill size). Light the paper in several places. Don't start cooking until the wood coals glow red under a coating of white ash, about 30 minutes. To check whether the coals are ready, hold the palm of your hand 5 or 6 inches above the grill. If you can tolerate the heat for only 3 or 4 seconds, your fire is ready. Don't rush!
   - As a cheap alternative to the all-wood fire, mound 10 to 15 briquets on a bed of crumbled newspapers, ignite, and let them burn down to red-hot coals, about 25 minutes. Add some vine clippings or wood chips just before grilling and throughout the cooking process. (Soak the chips in water first.)

3. Adjusting the heat: Food that's not browning needs a heat increase. But food that chars, blackens, or loses juices too quickly needs less heat. To get the heat just right:
   - Push coals closer together to increase heat output; spread them out to reduce it.
   - Also, raise the heat by opening the grill vents or lowering the grill height.
   - To reduce heat, simply do the reverse: close the vents and raise the grill.
   - Moving food to the center of the grill exposes it to higher temperatures; moving it to the periphery takes some heat off.

GRILLED GRAND MARNIER CHICKEN

Grand Marnier is a cognac-based orange liqueur.

6 servings

¾ cup Grand Marnier
1¼ cups apricot jam
¾ cup distilled white vinegar
4½ tablespoons Worcestershire sauce
3 tablespoons Dijon mustard
3 tablespoons honey
1 tablespoon dried red pepper flakes
3 whole chicken breasts (about 1 pound each), skinned, boned, and halved
Olive oil

1. In a saucepan, combine the Grand Marnier, jam, vinegar, Worcestershire sauce, mustard, honey, and red pepper flakes. Simmer over medium-low heat until the honey and jam are melted. Remove from the heat and let cool to room temperature.

2. Place the chicken breasts in a single layer in a shallow glass baking dish. Pour on the marinade and refrigerate, covered with plastic wrap, for at least 4 hours or overnight. Let the chicken stand at room temperature for half an hour before grilling.

3. Prepare a charcoal fire. When the coals are glowing hot with a layer of white ash, grill the chicken breasts 6 to 8 inches from the heat. Baste the breasts with oil during grilling. Cook for 20 minutes, turning every 5 minutes. Slice and serve hot or at room temperature.

SMOKING, SOAKING, AND BASTING FOR MORE FLAVOR

To produce more flavorful smoke from your grill, water-soak aromatic wood chips for 15 minutes and toss onto the coals. Moisture increases the smolder effect, sending more flavor up to the food. Or soak herbs, dried apples, or peaches and toss them onto the coals for extra-interesting aromatic smoke. Covering the grill for part of the cooking time creates even more intense flavor results.

Marinating foods in flavorful, slightly acidic liquids before grilling serves the threefold purpose of tenderizing, moisturizing (to prevent grill dry-out), and flavor enhancing. Even oil-based marinades add minimal calories, because most of the marinade drips off during grilling.

For a quick shot of flavor (without the 4 or more hours of marinating), infuse ½ cup olive oil with a generous tablespoon of chopped fresh herbs, orange peel, cracked pepper, red pepper flakes, cumin, or shallots. Brush on the chicken breasts before grilling for instant fantastic flavor.

For paillards, cutlets, or thin, boneless pieces of poultry, marinate for at least 30 minutes. Watch carefully and baste frequently while cooking, as they overcook easily.

SHERRY-MARINATED CHICKEN BREASTS

4–6 servings

3 whole chicken breasts (about 1 pound
    each), skinned, boned (optional),
    and halved
1½ cups dry sherry
3 tablespoons fresh lemon juice
1 bay leaf
2 large garlic cloves, pressed
1 cup finely chopped onion
1 15-ounce can tomato purée
3 tablespoons honey
2 tablespoons light molasses
1 teaspoon salt
½ teaspoon cayenne pepper
½ teaspoon dried thyme
½ teaspoon freshly ground black pepper
3 tablespoons white wine vinegar

POP YOUR TOAST ON THE GRILL!

Just about any bread benefits from grilling. Try thick slices of a crusty peasant loaf, baguette, pita pockets, corn bread, biscuits, or tortillas.

Lightly brush both sides of the bread with a fruity olive oil (using a bunch of herbs as a brush adds more flavor) and sprinkle with coarse salt. Rub slices with the cut side of a garlic clove, if desired. Grill over gentle heat on the perimeter, with the entree cooking in the center.

1. Place the chicken breasts in a shallow glass baking dish.

2. In a large bowl, combine the sherry, lemon juice, bay leaf, garlic, and onion. Pour over the chicken breasts and coat well. Refrigerate, covered with plastic wrap, at least 6 hours. Let the chicken stand at room temperature for half an hour before grilling.

3. Drain the chicken breasts, saving the marinade. In a heavy medium saucepan, combine the marinade with the tomato purée, honey, molasses, salt, cayenne, thyme, and black pepper. Bring to a boil over moderate heat, reduce the heat to low, and cook, stirring occasionally, until the sauce is thick and reduced to about 2 cups, 30 to 35 minutes. Remove from the heat, discard the bay leaf, and stir in the vinegar. Set aside.

4. Prepare a charcoal fire. When the coals are glowing with a layer of white ash, grill the chicken breasts about 6 to 8 inches from the heat. Turning and basting with the marinade every 3 to 5 minutes, cook for 20 minutes, or until done. Serve immediately or at room temperature.

GRILLED TANDOORI CHICKEN BREASTS AND VEGETABLES WITH MINTED-YOGURT SAUCE

4–6 servings

3 whole chicken breasts (about 1 pound each), skinned and flattened, left whole or halved
1¾ cups plain yogurt

Marinade
½ cup olive oil
¼ cup vinegar
1 3-inch piece of fresh ginger, peeled and cut into chunks
8 large garlic cloves, peeled
2 tablespoons ground cumin
2 tablespoons ground coriander
2 teaspoons ground cardamom
1½ teaspoons salt
1 teaspoon cayenne pepper
½ teaspoon ground cloves
2 tablespoons yellow food coloring (optional)

1 small cauliflower, cored, stemmed, and broken into large florets
2 to 4 medium carrots, peeled and quartered slantwise
2 onions, cut into ½-inch slices
1 to 2 zucchini, halved lengthwise

Yogurt Mint Sauce
1 plain yogurt
1 cucumber, peeled, seeded, and grated
2 tablespoons chopped fresh mint
Fresh cilantro sprigs for garnish
Thin lemon slices for garnish

1. Put the chicken breasts in a large bowl. Make slashes 1 inch apart along the grain. Push the yogurt into the slashes.

2. In a blender or a food processor fitted with a steel blade, combine the oil, vinegar, ginger, garlic, cumin, coriander, cardamom, salt, cayenne, cloves, and food coloring. Process to a purée.

3. Pour the marinade over the breasts. Turn several times to coat well, and push the marinade into the slashes. Refrigerate overnight, covered with plastic wrap, or marinate at room temperature at least 2 hours. Let the chicken stand at room temperature half an hour before grilling.

4. Prepare a charcoal fire. When the coals are glowing with a layer of white ash, scatter soaked grapevine cuttings over the coals and allow the heat to subside to a moderate level. Lightly brush the grilling racks with oil.

5. Remove the chicken breasts from the marinade and allow any excess to drain off. Brush the cauliflower, carrots, onions, and zucchini with the marinade and let dry.

6. Place the chicken breasts toward the center of the grill, the vegetables around the outer rim, and grill for 20 minutes, or until done, turning every 3 to 5 minutes. Do not overcook. Check the vegetables and turn frequently. They are done when slightly soft but not mushy. Do not let them burn.

7. Combine the yogurt, cucumber, and 1 tablespoon of the mint. Chill until time to serve. Just before serving, sprinkle with the remaining mint.

8. To serve, arrange the chicken breasts on a platter. Surround with the grilled vegetables, and decorate the platter with cilantro and lemon slices. Serve with yogurt sauce.

Q: When is a grilled chicken breast ready?

A: To grill perfectly, when the coals are glowing red hot and covered with a top layer of white ash, place the chicken breasts on the grill and cook for 5 minutes. (In some cases, it will be necessary to lightly oil the grill.) Turn several times during the 20-minute cooking process. To test for perfect doneness, pierce a breast with a knife. The meat should be white and slightly opaque throughout but still juicy. Do not overcook. Basting with a marinade during grilling helps to seal in the moisture and keep the chicken from drying out.

PATIENCE, PLEASE!

Mythology tells us mankind has been cooking food over glowing embers since Prometheus' time. The technique has reached a very high level of proficiency except for one typically American failing—lack of patience.

Patience is the primary ingredient for mastery of the grill—to wait for the coals to catch, for the flames to die down, for the slow roasting that will ensure aromatic, succulent, smoke-flavored food, which only grilling over coals can impart.

Timing, too, is crucial. The charcoal will not be ready to use for at least 30 minutes after the fire is started. There is no way this process can be speeded up, so allow yourself plenty of time. This can be leisure cooking at its best.

GRILLED CHICKEN BREASTS AND HERBED EGGPLANT WITH THYME CREAM SAUCE

6 servings

Juice of 1 lemon
¾ cup olive oil
¼ cup soy sauce
3 garlic cloves, peeled and crushed
½ teaspoon freshly ground black pepper
1 sprig each fresh marjoram, summer savory, and thyme
3 whole chicken breasts (about 1 pound each), skinned, boned, and halved
1 large eggplant, ends trimmed off, cut into 4 slices lengthwise
2 tablespoons finely chopped fresh rosemary
2 tablespoons crumbled dried oregano
Salt and freshly ground black pepper to taste
2 slices pancetta (Italian bacon)
1 teaspoon olive oil
1 pound pearl onions, boiled for 30 seconds, peeled, and cut in half lengthwise
8 fresh thyme sprigs
2 cups heavy cream
Chopped fresh thyme for garnish

1. In a small bowl, combine the lemon juice, half the oil, and the soy sauce, garlic, salt, and black pepper. Stir to mix well.

2. Pound or bruise the herbs lightly to release their oils, and mix into the marinade. Let stand, covered, 3 to 4 hours at room temperature, stirring occasionally.

3. Place the chicken breasts in a shallow glass baking dish. Prick both sides with a fork or the tip of a paring knife.

4. Strain the marinade and pour over the chicken, coating both sides well. Cover the dish with plastic wrap and refrigerate for 4 hours.

5. Brush the eggplant slices on both sides with the reserved marinade. Sprinkle on the rosemary, oregano, and salt and pepper. Cover with plastic wrap and set aside.

6. Cut the pancetta into ¼-inch pieces. In a sauté pan, sauté the pancetta in the olive oil over medium heat until well browned. Add the onions and continue cooking over low heat until they are translucent. Add the thyme sprigs and cream to the onion mixture. Reduce over medium heat by one quarter, season with black pepper and set aside.

7. Prepare a charcoal fire. When the fire is glowing with a layer of white ash, place the eggplant slices around the outer rim of the grill so they are not directly over the coals. Grill until slightly blackened and soft but not mushy, watching carefully so they do not burn. Turn once during grilling.

8. Remove the chicken from the marinade. Let the chicken stand at room temperature half an hour before grilling. Grill 6 to 8 inches from the coals for 20 minutes, turning every 5 minutes, until done.

9. Heat the sauce through. Place the eggplant slices on individual plates, spoon on the sauce, top with chicken breasts, and sprinkle on the chopped thyme. Serve the remaining sauce on the side.

GRILLED CHICKEN IN CUMIN MARINADE

6 servings

3 whole chicken breasts (about 1 pound each), skinned and flattened
Salt and freshly ground black pepper to taste
2 cups plain yogurt
¼ cup honey
2 tablespoons cumin seeds
1 tablespoon ground cumin
2 tablespoons dry mustard
4 tablespoons chopped fresh cilantro

1. Place the chicken breasts in a shallow glass baking dish. Sprinkle with salt and pepper.

2. In a bowl, combine the yogurt, honey, cumin seeds, ground cumin, and mustard.

3. Pour the marinade on the chicken breasts, coating both sides well. Refrigerate, covered, for at least 4 hours or overnight. Let the chicken stand half an hour at room temperature before grilling.

4. Prepare a charcoal fire. When the coals are glowing hot with a layer of white ash, grill the chicken breasts 6 to 8 inches from the heat. Turning every 5 minutes, cook for 20 minutes, or until done. Sprinkle with cilantro and serve.

CHICKEN RANCHERO

You've probably eaten eggs ranchero for breakfast. Ranchero style, in Texas or Mexico, simply means with tomato sauce of some particular type. This classic ranchero sauce recipe can be used for chip dipping as well.

4 servings

1 small onion, thinly sliced
1 large garlic clove, thinly sliced
½ cup chopped fresh cilantro
1 fresh jalapeño pepper, seeded and thinly sliced
1 ripe medium tomato, cored and thinly sliced
2 whole chicken breasts (about 1 pound each), halved and flattened to 1 inch thick
½ teaspoon salt and freshly ground black pepper

Salsa
2 large ripe juicy tomatoes (about 1 pound), cored and diced
¼ cup chopped cilantro
2 tablespoons minced white onion
1 small jalapeño pepper, seeded and minced
2 tablespoons olive oil
½ teaspoon salt
¼ teaspoon freshly ground black pepper
2 tablespoons fresh lemon juice

1. In a shallow glass baking dish, layer half the onion, garlic, cilantro, jalapeño, and sliced tomato. Season the chicken breasts with salt and pepper. Place on top of the ingredients in the baking dish. Cover with the remaining onion, garlic, cilantro, jalapeño, and tomato. Refrigerate, covered with plastic wrap, 12 hours or overnight. Let the chicken breasts stand at room temperature for half an hour before grilling.

2. For the salsa, in a mixing bowl, combine the diced tomatoes, cilantro, onion, jalapeño, oil, salt, pepper, and lemon juice. Cover with plastic wrap, and let stand at room temperature for 2 hours or in the refrigerator overnight. Serve at room temperature.

3. Prepare a charcoal fire. When the coals are glowing with a layer of white ash, place the chicken breasts on the grill, 6 to 8 inches from the heat. Turning every 5 minutes, grill for 20 minutes, or until done. Serve with salsa on the side.

GRILLED CHICKEN KABOBS

Sprinkle the fire with sprigs of herbs that have been soaked in water. This creates an even more intense flavor.

4 servings

2 whole chicken breasts (about 1 pound each), skinned, boned, and cut into 1½-inch strips
½ red bell pepper, stemmed, seeded, and cut into 2-inch pieces
½ green bell pepper, stemmed, seeded, and cut into 2-inch pieces
½ yellow bell pepper, stemmed, seeded, and cut into 2-inch pieces
¼ cup fresh lemon juice
¼ cup dry white wine
2 tablespoons grated lemon zest
3 shallots, chopped
3 garlic cloves, minced
2 tablespoons chopped fresh basil, or ½ teaspoon dried basil
3 tablespoons chopped fresh parsley
2 tablespoons chopped fresh marjoram, or ½ teaspoon dried marjoram
¼ teaspoon freshly ground white pepper
8 to 10 pearl onions (cut into the root end, boil for 30 seconds, and peel)
8 cherry tomatoes

1. Combine the chicken, bell peppers, lemon juice, wine, zest, shallots, garlic, basil, parsley, marjoram, and white pepper in a shallow glass baking dish. Marinate at room temperature for 1 hour or refrigerate, covered with plastic wrap, for at least 2 hours. Let stand at room temperature for half an hour before grilling the chicken.

2. Using 10 metal skewers, or bamboo skewers that have been soaked in water for 20 minutes, roll the drained chicken strips into pinwheel-like rounds and skewer, alternating them with pepper pieces, onions, and cherry tomatoes.

3. Prepare a charcoal fire. Lightly brush the grill with vegetable oil. When the coals are glowing with a layer of white ash, grill the kabobs 6 to 8 inches from the heat for 10 to 12 minutes, turning frequently. Serve immediately or at room temperature.

Q: **How should bone-in breasts be prepared so they lie flat on the grill?**

A: **When the breasts are left whole with the bone in, crack the bone to flatten it with a few strong smacks directly in the center (skinned side up, bone side on a flat, hard surface), using the palm of your hand or a heavy cast-iron skillet.**

GRILLED TERIYAKI CHICKEN

Remember, to perfectly marinate the chicken breasts you must leave them in the teriyaki sauce for 2–4 hours, so allow plenty of time in between marinating and cooking.

4 servings

2 whole chicken breasts (about 1 pound each), flattened and halved
¾ cup peeled and chopped fresh ginger
2 tablespoons minced garlic
½ cup sugar
1 cup sake
½ cup soy sauce

1. Place the breasts in a shallow glass baking dish.

2. In a blender or food processor fitted with a steel blade, combine the remaining ingredients. Process to a smooth purée.

3. Pour the marinade over the chicken breasts and coat well. Refrigerate, covered with plastic wrap, for at least 2–4 hours. Turn occasionally during marinating. Let stand half an hour before grilling.

4. Prepare a charcoal fire. When the coals are glowing with white ash, place the chicken breasts on the grill, 6 to 8 inches from the heat. Turning every 5 minutes, cook for 20 minutes, or until done. Serve immediately or at room temperature, sliced.

GRILLED FRUIT

Many fruits (except supersoft berries) do well by grilling. Their flavor intensifies, yet the sweetness is cut by the aromatic smoke. While fruit makes a spectacular ending to any grilled dinner, don't limit it to dessert. It's also a great condiment, quickly puréed into a side sauce for poultry. The basic technique is to brush fruits (halved peaches, nectarines, plums, papayas, apricots, or pears) with melted butter or light vegetable oil. Sprinkle with a dusting of nutmeg, ground cloves, or ground cinnamon. For easy handling, grill in a wire basket. Start testing for doneness (fruit should be soft but not mushy) after 3 to 5 minutes per side.

Other fruity grillables to try are apples (cored and cut into ½-inch rings) oranges, pineapple, mango (cut into ½-inch-thick slices), bananas (grilled whole in their peel for 5 minutes per side until very soft, then sliced open and scooped out).

Whole peaches, apples, nectarines, and apricots can be wrapped in foil and grilled directly on the coals. Cook about 20 minutes, turning occasionally.

MIXED GREENS WITH WARM JALAPENO VINAIGRETTE

Salad

1½ heads Boston lettuce
1 cup arugula
1 cup radicchio
2 bunches watercress, stems trimmed
2 fresh mint leaves, stems trimmed,
    chopped

Dressing

¼ cup vegetable oil
½ cup finely chopped onion
½ tablespoon chopped jalapeño peppers
    (stem, seed, and devein first)
¼ cup rice wine vinegar
1½ tablespoons honey
5 jalapeño peppers (optional), stemmed,
    seeded, deveined, and thinly sliced,
    for garnish

1. Wash the greens, spin dry, and tear into bite-size pieces. Divide evenly on 6 plates. Sprinkle on the mint.

2. In a small saucepan, heat the oil. Add the onion and chopped jalapeños, and cook over medium-high heat until the onion is translucent, about 3 minutes. Stir in the vinegar and honey.

3. Immediately pour the dressing over the salads, garnish with a few jalapeño slices, and serve immediately with grilled chicken breasts.

Note Romaine lettuce, Belgian endive, lamb's or field lettuce, baby red leaf lettuce, and red cabbage may also be used.

Q: When is it best to leave the bone and/ or skin intact?

A: Poaching with the skin and bone on the breast tends to give the meat more flavor and prevent toughness to some degree. When grilling, leaving on the bone and skin is optional and just a matter of taste. However, when the chicken breasts require flattening to ½ inch or less, the skin and bone must go.

THE PERFECT ACCOMPANIMENT— A SALAD ON THE SIDE

Simple marinated and grilled chicken breasts and an interesting assortment of salad greens on the side create the perfect low-cal meal. Here's an inspired salad combination, and it's dressed to kill!

CHICKEN BREASTS MARINATED IN AROMATIC HERBS

Outdoor eating under the stars—though you might experience an array of bugs performing kamikaze dives into your salad or sangria—nothing beats it for the experience. Somehow your cares slip away and the world looks lovely again. Add grilled herbed chicken breasts and vegetables and all will be well with the world once again.

6 servings

3 whole chicken breasts (about 1 pound each), skinned and flattened
3 tablespoons chopped fresh cilantro
3 tablespoons chopped fresh parsley
1½ garlic cloves, peeled
1 teaspoon ground paprika
¼ teaspoon ground cumin
⅛ teaspoon cayenne pepper
3 tablespoons fresh lemon juice
1 teaspoon salt
½ teaspoon freshly ground black pepper
¼ cup olive oil

1. Place the chicken breasts in a single layer in a shallow glass baking dish.

2. In a blender or a food processor fitted with a steel blade, combine the cilantro, parsley, garlic, paprika, cumin, cayenne, lemon juice, salt, and pepper. With the machine running, pour in the oil.

3. Pat the marinade onto both sides of the chicken breasts. Refrigerate, covered with plastic wrap, 4 to 6 hours. Let the chicken stand at room temperature for half an hour before grilling.

4. Prepare a charcoal fire. Remove the chicken breasts from the marinade and season with salt and pepper. When the coals are glowing with a layer of white ash, grill the chicken breasts 6 to 8 inches from the heat for 20 minutes, or until done, turning every 5 minutes. Serve immediately or at room temperature.

COLD SMOKED CHICKEN BREASTS WITH THREE-PEPPER COULIS

Simple grilled chicken breasts and a dollop of tasty sauce make a wonderful starter or lunch. For dinner, make an assortment of grilled vegetables as a side dish. To give it a Mexican or southwestern flavor, brush the vegetables with hot chile oil and serve the chicken breasts with salsa.

6 servings

2 cups dry white wine
¼ cup chopped fresh rosemary
2 or 3 garlic cloves, minced
Salt and freshly ground black pepper to taste
3 whole chicken breasts (about 1 pound each), flattened

Coulis
1 red bell pepper, seeded and chopped
1 green bell pepper, seeded and chopped
1 orange bell pepper, seeded and chopped
1 cup fresh cilantro
¼ cup olive oil

1. In a bowl, combine the wine, rosemary, garlic, and salt and pepper. Place the chicken breasts in a shallow glass baking dish. Pour the marinade over the chicken breasts. Refrigerate, covered with plastic wrap, for 12 hours, turning several times. Let stand at room temperature for half an hour before grilling.

2. In a blender or a food processor fitted with a steel blade, combine the bell peppers, cilantro, and oil. Blend to a fine purée. Press through a fine sieve and chill until ready to serve.

3. Prepare a charcoal fire. Add aromatic hardwood chunks that have been soaked in water for 2 hours.

4. Remove the chicken breasts from the marinade and pour the remaining marinade into the smoker pan. Place the chicken on a rack over the smoker pan and put the pan in place. Cover the smoker and cook 45 minutes to 1 hour, or until the chicken is opaque throughout. Test after 35 minutes by cutting into a breast along the bone. When done, refrigerate and serve cold with the coulis.

GRILLED GREENS AND OTHER VEGGIES

When it comes to grilling vegetables, you can cook them on the grill, and some right in the coals, at the same time as your entree.

All grilled vegetables should be brushed with oil before hitting the rack. Heartier greens like radicchio and endive not only stand up to but sweeten with grilling. Slice radicchio and endive in half lengthwise, brush with oil, and grill about 4 to 5 minutes per side. Slice tomatoes in half crosswise, brush with olive oil, sprinkle with herbs, and grill about 2 minutes per side. Grill corn on the cob right in the husk. Carefully peel the husk back, remove the silk, replace the husk, and soak 10 minutes in cold water. Then grill 15 minutes, turning frequently.

Baby veggies (or standard-size varieties, sliced ½ or ¾ inch thick) are also very grillable. Place in wire baskets and grill about 4 to 5 minutes on each side.

Root vegetables (potatoes, sweet potatoes, onions) taste best when cooked right in the coals. Just brush with oil, wrap in a double layer of heavy-duty foil ventilated with a few punched holes, and bury in the coals. Most cook tender in 45 minutes.

WHAT'S THAT SMOKING?

It's none other than mozzarella cheese. Just wrap a fresh mozzarella in aluminum foil and smoke for 2 to 3 hours. The fire should be very low. Use hickory, apple, mesquite, and other wood chunks and chips along with the charcoal.

For smoking, it is very important the fire be as low as possible, giving off almost no heat, just smoke. Soak wood chips in water for 30 minutes and add to the smoker from time to time during the 2- to 3-hour smoking time. The cheese will melt slightly. Mold it back into a round with your hands while still warm, then chill for several hours. Cut into ¼-inch slices and serve with ripe tomatoes, fresh oregano, and basil, drizzled with extra-virgin olive oil.

Also, consider smoking whole tomatoes, whole heads of garlic, onions, bell peppers, and even bread slices. They usually smoke in 30 minutes, and need to be turned. (Make a tomato sauce of the smoked tomatoes. The taste difference will be surprising, especially on pasta or a pizza.)

Microwaving

The New Wave in culinary creativity

To microwave or not to microwave— this is no longer the question! With over 80 percent of homes across the country including one of these devices, microwave cooking is here to stay.

But let's take a vote. What do you think of microwave cooking? In a pinch, is it an alternative to takeout, or great for people who like their water boiled fast? Yes, to all those thoughts, though there's more, especially when it involves chicken breasts.

A microwave oven can cook up a wonderfully succulent chicken breast along with a magnificent sauce in just a few minutes. Yes, it's a time-saver; though the variety of microwave chicken breast recipes is rather limited, here are several good things to set before your king or queen, or yourself, for that matter.

MICROWAVE CHICKEN STOCK

In my first book, *Chicken Breasts,* you'll find the perfect chicken stock recipes on pages 11 and 36. You can now add this time-saving variation to the collection. It is almost as flavorful as long-cooked stock.

3 cups

3 pounds chicken parts, including backs, necks, and bones
1 carrot, peeled and coarsely chopped
1 small onion, quartered
2 celery stalks, coarsely chopped
¼ cup minced fresh parsley
1 bay leaf
4 peppercorns
¼ teaspoon dried thyme
4 cups water

1. Combine all the ingredients in a 3-quart microwave-proof bowl.

2. Cover and cook on full power for 20 minutes. Skim off any scum that collects on top of the stock during cooking.

3. Reduce the power to medium and cook 1 hour more.

4. Strain through a sieve or colander lined with dampened cheesecloth.

Note The stock can be refrigerated, covered, for up to 3 days. Remove the layer of fat from the surface before using. Remember, never add salt, ground pepper, or other seasonings to stock. Seasonings are added to the finished dish of which the stock is a part.

Q: How should chicken breasts be arranged in order to cook evenly in the microwave oven?

A: The food closest to the outside of the dish cooks fastest. If you have uneven pieces of chicken, place the thickest ends at the edges of the plate. A carousel usually offers even cooking throughout.

MICROWAVE POACHED CHICKEN BREASTS

With just this one recipe, an endless array of chicken dinner combinations can be achieved. This is a *basic* microwave chicken breast. (See sauces to follow.)

6 servings

3 whole chicken breasts (about 1 pound each), skinned, boned, and split
¼ cup chicken stock (see page 9)
¼ cup dry white wine
1 tablespoon chopped fresh tarragon
Salt and freshly ground white pepper to taste

1. Arrange the chicken breasts in a microwave-proof dish, centering the thin ends together. Pour on the stock and wine and sprinkle with tarragon and salt and pepper.

2. Cover the dish tightly with microwave plastic wrap. Cook on high for 8 minutes.

3. Serve with the pan juices or a sauce of your choice.

Q: Does reheating chicken breasts in the microwave make them tough?

A: Not really. To reheat, add a few drops of water to the dish containing the chicken breasts and cover with microwavable plastic wrap. Reheat no longer than absolutely necessary.

MICROWAVE VELOUTE SAUCE FOR QUICK OR POACHED CHICKEN BREASTS

This is a sauce that easily adapts to microwave cooking. See the variations for more ideas.

2½ tablespoons unsalted butter
3 tablespoons all-purpose flour
1½ cups chicken stock (see page 9)
½ cup heavy cream
1 tablespoon lemon juice or a splash of
    sweet or dry vermouth (optional)
Salt and freshly ground white pepper to
    taste

1. In a microwave-proof 1-quart dish, heat the butter for ½ minute on full power or until melted.

2. Whisk in the flour. Slowly add the chicken stock and cream, whisking continuously until completely combined. Cook for 5 minutes on full power, stirring every 2 minutes.

3. The sauce is done when it coats the back of a spoon. Whisk in the lemon juice. Add salt and pepper. Serve immediately.

VARIATIONS

Fresh Herb Velouté Add ½ cup fresh chopped herbs in step 2.

Curry Velouté Add 1 to 2 teaspoons curry powder, or to taste, with the flour.

Sauce Supreme Increase the butter to 6 tablespoons and add 3 tablespoons each very finely minced carrot, onion, and celery. Reduce the stock to 1 cup. Increase the cream to 1 cup and add 2 tablespoons dry white wine.

Roasted-Garlic Velouté Add 1 whole head of garlic, top trimmed to expose the top of each clove. Put the garlic and 2 tablespoons chicken stock in a 4-cup glass dish. Drizzle 1½ tablespoons olive oil over the garlic. Cover tightly with microwave plastic wrap. Cook on full power for 6 to 8 minutes, cooking longer if the bulbs are very large (like elephant garlic). Remove from the oven and let stand 10 minutes. Scoop out the buttery garlic and stir it into the finished velouté.

QUICK MICROWAVE CHICKEN BREASTS

Chill the cooked chicken and combine with salad ingredients or a pasta of your choice, or stir up a chicken à la king.

4 servings

2 whole chicken breasts (about 1 pound each), skinned, boned, and cut into 1-inch cubes
2 tablespoons fresh lemon juice
1 teaspoon paprika
Salt and freshly ground black pepper to taste

1. Place the chicken breasts microwave-proof casserole d. ... sprinkle with the lemon juice, paprika, and salt and pepper. Stir to coat the chicken breasts.

2. Stirring every 2 minutes to baste, cover and microwave on high for 6 minutes, or until the chicken is no longer pink.

3. Remove the chicken breasts with a slotted spoon. Serve combined with a sauce or other ingredients.

CHICKEN BREASTS WITH LIME AND CILANTRO

4 servings

2 whole chicken breasts (about 1 pound each), skinned, boned, and halved
1 tablespoon fresh lime juice
Salt and freshly ground black pepper to taste
1 tablespoon chopped fresh cilantro

1. Place the chicken breasts in a shallow glass casserole. Sprinkle with lime juice and salt and pepper.

2. Cover and microwave on high for 6 minutes, or until the chicken breasts are no longer pink. Halfway through the cooking time, turn the lesser-cooked portions toward the edges of the casserole.

3. Sprinkle with cilantro and serve.

CHICKEN, PROSCIUTTO, AND PARMESAN RISOTTO

When risotto is done, it's done. So be ready, forks in place, to eat immediately. If cooked the conventional way, risotto takes about 30 minutes from start to finish, with someone attending the pot for the entire time. Risotto in the microwave requires no arm-aching antics and comes out great. Test your imagination when it comes to variations. Almost anything from mushrooms to tender peas can be added to this Italian wonder.

2 servings

1 whole chicken breast (about 1 pound), skinned, boned, and trimmed of excess fat
1 tablespoon olive oil
2 shallots, minced
1 cup finely chopped leeks (white part and some green)
1 cup Arborio rice (Italian rice—do not substitute other types)
3 cups chicken stock (see page 9)
⅔ cup dry white wine
½ teaspoon salt
¼ teaspoon freshly ground white pepper

4 tablespoons chopped prosciutto, sautéed for 3 minutes in a scant amount of olive oil
1 to 2 teaspoons unsalted butter
¾ cup grated Parmesan cheese (Roggerio or other fresh Parmesan, imported or domestic)
2 tablespoons snipped fresh chives
Freshly ground black pepper

1. Shred the chicken breast across the grain into thin pieces (it should equal at least 1 cup). Set aside.

2. In a microwave-proof 2-quart casserole, heat the oil for 1 minute on full power.

3. Add the shallots and leeks. Cook 3 minutes on full power.

4. Add the rice and stir to mix well. Cook 1 minute more on full power.

5. Add ½ cup of the stock and the wine, salt, and pepper. Cook for 12 minutes on full power, uncovered.

6. Stir in the remaining stock and the chicken and prosciutto. Cook 4 minutes on full power. Stir in the butter and continue cooking 1 minute.

7. Add the cheese and stir to combine well. Place the risotto in the center of a shallow soup plate and sprinkle on the chives. Pass the pepper mill and more Parmesan cheese on the side.

VARIATION Bacon, Olive, and Mushroom Risotto. Use Italian black and green slivered olives, dried wild mushrooms that have been reconstituted in your favorite red or white wine (add the wine to the liquid), Canadian bacon, or white or black truffles for special risotto dinners.

CHICKEN AND DIJON MUSTARD SAUCE

Try this over your favorite pasta.

2–4 servings

1 cup milk
½ cup heavy cream
3 to 4 tablespoons Dijon mustard
2 teaspoons fresh lemon juice

Salt and freshly ground white pepper to taste

2½ cups Quick Microwave Chicken chunks (see page 121)

1 tablespoon chopped fresh parsley

1. Combine all ingredients, except the chicken and parsley, in an 8-cup glass measuring cup.

2. Cook, uncovered, for 11 minutes at full power.

3. Combine the chicken with the sauce and cook 1 minute on high. Add the parsley for the last minute of cooking. Serve immediately.

CHICKEN BREASTS WITH TARRAGON BUTTER

4 servings

4 tablespoon unsalted butter
2 tablespoons chopped fresh tarragon, or
    2 teaspoons dried tarragon
2 whole chicken breasts (about 1 pound
    each), skinned, boned, and flattened
    to 1 inch thick
3 tablespoons fresh lemon juice

1. Place the butter on a sheet of waxed paper. Microwave on low or defrost for 15 seconds, or just until soft. Roll the butter in tarragon and form a stick or cylinder. Wrap and chill until ready to use.

2. Place the chicken breasts in a microwave-proof shallow 10-inch round dish, with the thickest portions toward the edges; keep the center of the dish open. Sprinkle the chicken breasts with lemon juice. Cover loosely with microwave plastic wrap that has been pierced with a fork.

3. Cook on medium power for 7 minutes. Turn over and place the less-cooked portions toward the edges of the baking dish. Cook 7 minutes longer, or until the flesh is firm to the touch. For the last minute of cooking time, place pats of tarragon butter on each breast. Serve with another pat on each.

Index